HOW TO MAKE
YOUR OWN KNIVES

HOW TO MAKE YOUR OWN KNIVES

Knife-making for the Home Hobbyist

by Jim Mayes

Illustrated by Dale Bolen

EVEREST HOUSE
Publishers New York

To Barbara . . .

Who allows me to spend more time than I should at the workbench.

Copyright © 1978 by James H. Mayes, Jr.
All Rights Reserved
ISBN: 0-89696-146-X
Library of Congress Catalog Card Number: 78-57407

Published simultaneously in
Canada by Beaverbooks,
Don Mills, Ontario

Printed in the United States of America

TABLE OF CONTENTS

FOREWORD   9

CHAPTER 1 **A BRIEF HISTORY OF KNIVES AND KNIFE-MAKING**   13

CHAPTER 2 **KNIFE NOMENCLATURE: What to Call That Thingamabob**   24

CHAPTER 3 **UNDERSTANDING METALLURGY: The Steel-Maker's Art**   29

CHAPTER 4 **SETTING UP YOUR WORKBENCH**   38

CHAPTER 5 **GETTING STARTED: Where There's a Will, There's a Knife**   48

CHAPTER 6 **BLADE DESIGN: Sizes, Shapes, and Grinds**   56

CHAPTER 7	**THE BLADE:** Getting What You Want in a Handmade Knife	65
CHAPTER 8	**HEAT TREATMENT:** Giving Your Blade Its Character	75
CHAPTER 9	**THE TANG:** Its Purpose and Design	82
CHAPTER 10	**HILTS AND POMMELS:** How to Make Them	87
CHAPTER 11	**THE HANDLE:** An Expression of Your Individuality	105
CHAPTER 12	**EPOXY AND HOW TO USE IT**	124
CHAPTER 13	**USING PINS AND CUTLER'S RIVETS**	131
CHAPTER 14	**FINISHING YOUR KNIFE:** Sanding, Buffing, and Polishing	141
CHAPTER 15	**THE SHEATH:** How to Design and Make It	151

CHAPTER 16	**KNIFE CARE:** Honing and Other Thoughts	**166**
APPENDIX	**Glossary of Knife-Making Terms**	**179**
	Where to Order What You Need	**188**
	Knife-Making Supplies and Services	**190**

FOREWORD

This is obviously another one of those how-to-do-it books. That's what it's meant to be and that's what it is. But I hope the information it contains will also instill in you, as it has in me, a greater appreciation of the art and science that is knife-making in America today.

By reading this book and following the instructions it offers, you will be reliving a heritage that is older than our country itself. I believe you will discover, too, the pleasure of melding metals, woods, stag, and other components into practical artistry. You will find that the only limitations imposed on your ability to produce fine cutlery are the time and care with which you approach this satisfying hobby.

I make no pretense that all of the information contained herein is original. Indeed, many of the most useful tricks I have learned have been those taught to me by others. At the same time, I am sure that some of the statements I make will not be accepted by every knife-maker. For this I take full blame, and say only that this is part of the fun of knife-making.

This book above all else, is intended to be practical. There is no statement made and no lesson taught that is based on hearsay. Everything has been tried in my basement workshop. The suppliers I list and recommend are those who have provided satisfactory service and materials to me at competitive prices. I apologize in advance to any who might be offended by my omitting them.

Through words, photographs, and illustrations, I have attempted to chronicle the step-by-step approach I have found most useful during the several years I have been making knives as a home hobbyist. I have not tried to gloss over difficult tasks, nor have I made some jobs seem more difficult than they really are.

With the possible exception of the chapters on metallurgy and heat treatment, I have not used technical terms that are beyond the understanding of the average hobbyist. Terms and language that are somewhat specialized are explained in the text or in a glossary at the end of the book.

On the assumption that the reader of this book is, like me, an outdoorsman entering upon knife-making largely because he admires quality workmanship and seeks something "a little out of the ordinary," I have included a chapter on the history of knives and knife-making, and discussed briefly the background of some of America's great custom knife-makers. Other books have done this quite well, however, and my real purpose in this book is to help the reader become proficient in knife-making with tools and material that are readily available.

If this book inspires you to join the thousands who enjoy using, collecting, and showing knives that are the product of their own skill and imagination, then I have done what I set out to do.

Jim Mayes
Homewood, Illinois
May 1978

HOW TO MAKE YOUR OWN KNIVES

CHAPTER 1

A BRIEF HISTORY OF KNIVES AND KNIFE-MAKING

Today's knife-maker—whether hobbyist or professional—is recreating a form of craftsmanship that began in Asia and Europe many centuries ago, traveled to America with the earliest pioneers, crossed the Alleghenies and later the Rockies with the first westward migrations, and finally became entrenched among frontier blacksmiths as a distinctly American art and craft.

In common with the early day gunsmiths of New England and Pennsylvania, the pioneer knife-makers created a utilitarian art form that blossomed for a while, succumbed to mass production for about a century, then again fluttered to life about four decades ago.

Today's knife-makers, many of them working on home workbenches, are creating some of the finest knives the world has ever known. Almost without exception, the most indistinctive knife today contains steel that would have turned our forebears green with envy.

The history of knife-making is the history of mankind itself. The very earliest relics found in association with ancient man include edged weapons with which those primitive folk sought to defend themselves, and used to provide food, clothing, and shelter for their families.

No one can pinpoint when the first crude flint knife was made, but for most of human history it has been man's basic tool. Bronze knives were made in Asia and along the Mediterranean seacoast at least 5,000 years ago, and the first iron knife blade was probably pounded out of a meteor not too many years later. True ironwork began in Turkey about 1100 BC and intricately designed knives have been dated from that period. Southern Europeans learned to make blades from iron long before the northern countries and the early Romans carried that knowledge with them to England and Scotland.

Pioneer American Knifesmith

Knife-making as a distinctly American art and craft became entrenched among early pioneer blacksmiths, then moved westward with early migrations that swept across the Alleghenies and later the Rockies.

Although mythology is steeped in tales of fantastically good blades used by the early Greeks, Romans, Turks, and others, no steel of consistent quality was produced until the middle 1700s. Until this point in history, steel-making was largely a hit-or-miss proposition—some batches might well have been exceptional, others hardly qualified as good pot-making metal.

Throughout the Middle Ages and the Renaissance, daggers and short swords were as much an article of dress as a man's boots. No well dressed member of the upper class would have dreamed of venturing forth without a trusted blade at his side. As we shall see in the chapter on blade design, those early swords and daggers have influenced modern design.

THE SHEFFIELD AND SOLINGEN INFLUENCE

By the late 1700s, fine knives were being produced in many parts of the civilized world, but particularly in England and Germany. Blades forged and ground in Sheffield (England) and Solingen (Germany) came to be identified as cutlery of superior quality. Both cities retain that reputation even today, and some of the best blades being used by modern American knife-makers have their origin in those places.

At about the same time that Sheffield and Solingen were earning reputations as mass producers of fine cutlery, frontier blacksmiths in America were producing blades of limited number but excellent quality. From the time the Pilgrims landed in America until the industrial revolution of the mid-1800s, most of the knives used in America continued to be supplied by English and European cutlers. European, and particularly English, knives were important trade items for bartering with western Indian tribes as pioneers crossed the Mississippi and began their settlement of the West.

The Western settlers and the fur trappers who preceded them, tended to regard their knives as strictly utilitarian objects, and only isolated efforts were made to supply knives of superior quality. With notable exceptions, even the custom-forged blades of that day were crude affairs compared to today's standards.

A small group of American manufacturers, mostly located in the New England states, did spring up to satisfy the utilitarian market of the late 1700s and early 1800s. Among them were the Harrington Cutlery Company, founded in 1818, and the John Russell Cutlery Company, founded in 1834.

Strangely enough, these two early New England companies are today merged, and still doing business as the Russell Harrington Cutlery Company. The John Russell Company in particular, became known throughout the West for its brand of Green River knives, a trademark that continues to this day. Literally thousands of these relatively crude but sturdy knives were used by the early fur trappers, mountain men, and buffalo hunters. A kind of "kit," composed of ripper, skinner, and sharpening steel or stone contained in a soft-leather pouch, was widely used on the western plains to satisfy the Eastern and European market for buffalo hides.

Buffalo skinner with inlet stag grips is backed by another weapon of its era, a cap-and-ball Navy Colt with original leatherwork by author. The blade, an original from the John Russell Company, is from Indian Ridge Traders and sambar stag scales are from E. Christopher Firearms Company. The original Russell knives used beechwood almost exclusively as handle material.

The vast majority of early American-made knives were simple, full-tang instruments with straight wooden handles, usually of birch or hickory, but sometimes (in higher-priced knives) of more exotic woods such as ebony and rosewood. The earliest versions of these knives, made by the John Russell Company and others, used pins to anchor their scale handles to the tang. Later models used cutler's rivets, sometimes alone or in combination with pins.

Hollywood to the contrary, guards (or hilts) were seldom seen on early frontier knives, and those knives on which they did appear were invariably made in England or custom-designed for their intended owners.

THE BOWIE LEGEND — MAN AND KNIFE

Then in a period of little more than a decade, the design of American-made knives (and subsequently, English-made as well) was changed through the efforts of an obscure Arkansas blacksmith named James Black and a frontier adventurer named Jim Bowie. The story of the Bowie knife, whose design influenced American knifemaking for more than a century, has been told many times and in many ways. Down in Texas, we tell it something like this:

In the late 1820s following some unpleasantness ensuing from a duel in his native state of Louisiana, Bowie moved to Texas which was then a province of Mexico, where he settled in San Antonio and soon became a respected member of that frontier society.

Three or four years later Bowie traveled back East on business, and passed through the southwestern Arkansas town of Washington. Now a tiny hamlet about 10 miles north of Hope, Arkansas, Washington in those days was a thriving city of some 5,000 residents. Bowie somehow heard of James Black, a local blacksmith and sometimes knife-maker, whose shop was located in Washington. (Restored today, it is a center of attraction.)

Legend recounts that Bowie presented Black a

wooden model of the fighting knife he wanted made and then continued on his journey east. When Bowie returned several weeks later, bound again for Texas, Black had made two knives—one of which followed Bowie's design faithfully, and the other representing Black's own notion of what a fighting knife should look like. Bowie, again according to legend, accepted Black's version over his own, and thus, the Bowie knife was born.

Not long after acquiring his new knife, which he is alleged to have worn even in polite society, Bowie was set upon by three highwaymen while traveling the Natchez Trace, an important military and commercial route that ran from Nashville, Tennessee, to Natchez, Mississippi. Using his knife as his primary weapon (Colt's invention of the repeating pistol was several years in the future), Bowie promptly dispatched all three of his assailants. The Bowie legend—man and knife—was firmly established.

Soon men all along the frontier were asking for knives "just like Jim Bowie's." Frontier blacksmiths did what they could to supply the burgeoning demand, but far more Bowie knives were actually imported from England than were ever made in this country. It was the importation of these knives that made such Sheffield firms as Joseph Rodgers and I-XL (the quixotic trade name used by George Wostenhold & Sons to this day) known throughout the American West.

As every Texas schoolboy knows, Jim Bowie immortalized himself forever by dying in defense of the Alamo on March 6, 1836. Strange though it seems, no trace of the original Bowie knife has ever been found. Nor have extensive searches ever turned up any other blade that could, without question, be attributed to the hand of James Black, the extraordinary Arkansas blacksmith who started it all.

Perhaps it is just as well. During the past century and a half, literally thousands of knives produced by scores of knife-makers have laid claim to being "just like Jim Bowie's." It would seem a shame for the original blade to be found and prove them wrong.

If historians are right, the first Bowie knife possessed a double guard, a broad swedged blade, and a relatively straight handle of bone or hard wood. The blade is believed to have been approximately 12 inches long and about two and a half or three inches wide. The overall length of the knife was probably about 16 or 17 inches. Altogether, a formidable weapon.

Some of our latter-day "Bowies" probably came very close to the original design; others undoubtedly would be unrecognized by James Black himself. Certainly if "wall hangers" are appealing to you, you'll likely want to try your hand at making what may well be the spittin' image of the most famous fighting knife of all times. No one can prove you wrong.

THE REBIRTH OF HANDMADE KNIVES

After reaching its zenith in the mid-19th century, knife-making in America began a slow but steady decline until its nadir was reached in the early years of this century. Although the making of fine knives never actually died out in this country, kept alive as it was by a few master cutlers, it was for a period of 40 or 50 years a mighty sick patient.

With most of the wilderness conquered, the Indian vanquished, and the buffalo decimated, the mass-produced knife became more abomination than blessing. Case, Ka-Bar, and a handful of other American companies refused to knuckle under to a flood of cheaply produced, foreign-made products, but the number of really good knives produced in the U.S. was pitifully few.

My 1902 (replica) edition of the Sears, Roebuck catalogue—said to represent the wants and aspirations of middle America—lists only five knives that could even be roughly construed as sporting or fighting models. The most expensive of these, something resembling a Bowie with a "deer foot" handle but called a "hunting" knife, listed for $1.50. Undoubtedly it was imported.

An "Arkansas" Bowie (whatever that may have been) listed for 95 cents, and a "ladies'

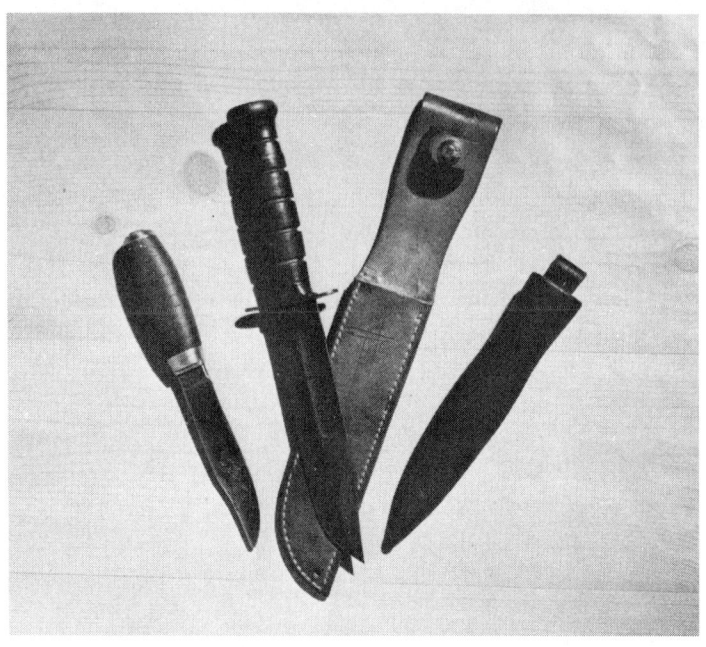

Typical of the knives made by American manufacturers during the Depression years of the '30s and the war years of the '40s are this hiltless hunter with tube sheath (left and right) produced by Marble about 1935, and the Marine Corps knife made by Ka-Bar during World War II (A. L. White collection).

pearl-handled dagger" went for $1.25. Thus, as the new century began, this altogether uninspiring picture of American tastes in straight knives emerged.

The disinterest of the early part of the 20th century gave way to the poverty of the '30s, when even the cheap imports found few takers. To be sure, every youngster had his prized 50-cent jackknife, and most men carried penknives or Barlows, depending upon their calling. But the straight sheath knife belonged to the past, only Boy Scouts and avid outdoorsmen carried them. We'd become too sophisticated (and too broke) for that sort of thing.

Predicated largely on our inability to buy decent straight knives at hardware or sporting goods store, some of us turned to making our own knives from files, sawblades, and sundry other bits of scrap metal. Some were surprisingly good, but often more by accident than by design.

Ah, but the flame of pride still flickered in some men's hearts. A few wealthy patrons of fine cutlery kept a handful of part-time custom cutlers from starving, and here and there a real master emerged. Around 1910, a man named William Scagel began turning out a few handmade knives up in the Michigan wilderness. Today, of course, his few remaining works are among the most avidly sought by collectors, and the prices they fetch would have kept old Bill in beans for many a day.

In his later years Scagel (who died in 1963 at a ripe old age) became something of a recluse. A long-forgotten dispute with the local power company left Bill without electricity, and so he fashioned an intricate system of belts and pulleys tied to an ancient gasoline engine which powered his saws, grinders, and sanders.

Many years before and after Scagel's time, scaled-down "Bowie" knives (with deer-foot handles, no less) were what passed for hunting knives. Scagel changed that by making blades to fit the purpose. It has been said that his skinning blades and caping knives are like extensions of the user's own hand.

Bill Scagel not only left an indelible mark on American knife-making, he also inspired others to follow in his footsteps. The first knife made by the famous Walter D. "Bo" Randall of Orlando, Florida, was an effort to copy a Scagel blade he saw being used to scrape the barnacles from the bottom of an old fishing boat.

Randall, more than any other man, can be said to be responsible for the rebirth of knife-making in this country. An avid outdoorsman, he began making knives professionally for servicemen during World War II. These same soldiers and marines, returned from war, sought but were unable to find, well-made hunting knives. This launched Randall's continuing career as one of America's preeminent custom knife-makers.

Today, the Randall catalogue lists nearly 30 different models of fighting and sporting knives, and his works are known and respected throughout the world. Randall knives have been carried by America's astronauts, bought by foreign potentates, and found their place in museums as objects of contemporary art and craftsmanship.

The Cooper Knife, now made in Burbank,

California is probably the oldest continually made line of custom-made knives in America today. Beginning in 1924, when John Nelson Cooper began grinding knives as a hobby for his friends in Tremont, Pennsylvania, the Cooper knive has become one of the nation's most highly respected lines. Cooper has specialized in recent years in making knives for collectors and Hollywood celebrities, but some excellent (if high priced) working knives still are offered.

The late Harry Morseth is another whose name must be counted among those responsible for the rebirth of handcrafted knives in America. Though Morseth died a few years ago, the business he began in 1934—making blades from a special laminated Norwegian steel—has today earned for the small northwestern Arkansas town of Springdale the sobriquet of "Knife Capital, USA." Now directed by another knife-smith named A. G. Russell, the business is, I believe, second only to Randall's in the number of handmade knives produced for American sportsmen.

During the past 10 or 15 years, the number of professional knife-makers in this country has proliferated. The official publication of the Knifemakers Guild of America lists more than 100 men whose careers are devoted to knife-making. Many of them, needless to say, began as home hobbyists, and gradually honed their skills as they honed their blades.

If the only dividing line between the amateur and the professional is whether the products he makes are good enough to merit sale to others, I'm sure their are hundreds, perhaps thousands, of home hobbyists who qualify today as professionals.

Thus, it has been a combination of factors—a growing appreciation of really fine cutlery, the desire to own something truly unique, a dissatisfaction with "store-bought" products, and perhaps a strong sense of nostalgia—that has led to the rebirth of knife-making in America. These same factors, to which must be added the sense of personal accomplishment, have given birth to knife-making as an art and craft to be practiced by the home hobbyist.

In response to this new, yet old avocation, a number of knife-makers' supply houses, catering to the wants and needs of hobbyists and professionals alike, have come into being. These suppliers, as we shall find in later chapters, are well prepared to provide for you—the home hobbyist—every item and accessory you will require to make your hobby practical, enjoyable, and—should you so desire—profitable as well.

Today, knife-making in America has come full circle, and picked up many important attributes along the way. Today, as it was two centuries ago, knife-making is a solid expression of man's search for individuality.

CHAPTER 2

KNIFE NOMENCLATURE: What to Call That Thingamabob

Like roses, it's easy to assume that a knife is a knife is a knife. Well, yes and no. All knives obviously have two major parts—the *blade** and the *handle*. One you hold and the other you cut with. Not much confusion up to this point. Or is there?

One small point we really should clear up right away is that swords have *hilts*, but not handles; knives have both hilt and handle. On a sword, everything above the blade is the hilt. On a knife, the hilt is synonomous with the *guard*, and above that (once the knife is assembled) we have the handle and the *pommel* or *butt cap*.

The purpose of the hilt, or guard, is to keep the user's hand from sliding down on the blade at inopportune times. Some knives have hilts, others don't. Additionally, some handles are constructed in such a way that the hilt is integral with the handle.

*Italicized words are defined in the glossary.

Every hilt, except those that are integral with the handle, has one or two crossbars extending out from it. If a single crossbar, called a *quillon*, is present, the hilt is referred to as being *single*. If two quillons are present, you have a *double* hilt.

Hilts languished in popularity for many years, only to again become popular when James Black invented the Bowie knife. The Bowie, and most other fighting knives, have double hilts (two quillons) for maximum protection of the user in hand-to-hand combat. Double hilts are a real nuisance on hunting knives, which are designed primarily for skinning, slicing, and caping. An additional advantage of the single hilt (one quillon) is that pouch-type sheaths which better protect the knife can be designed around them.

Knife Nomenclature

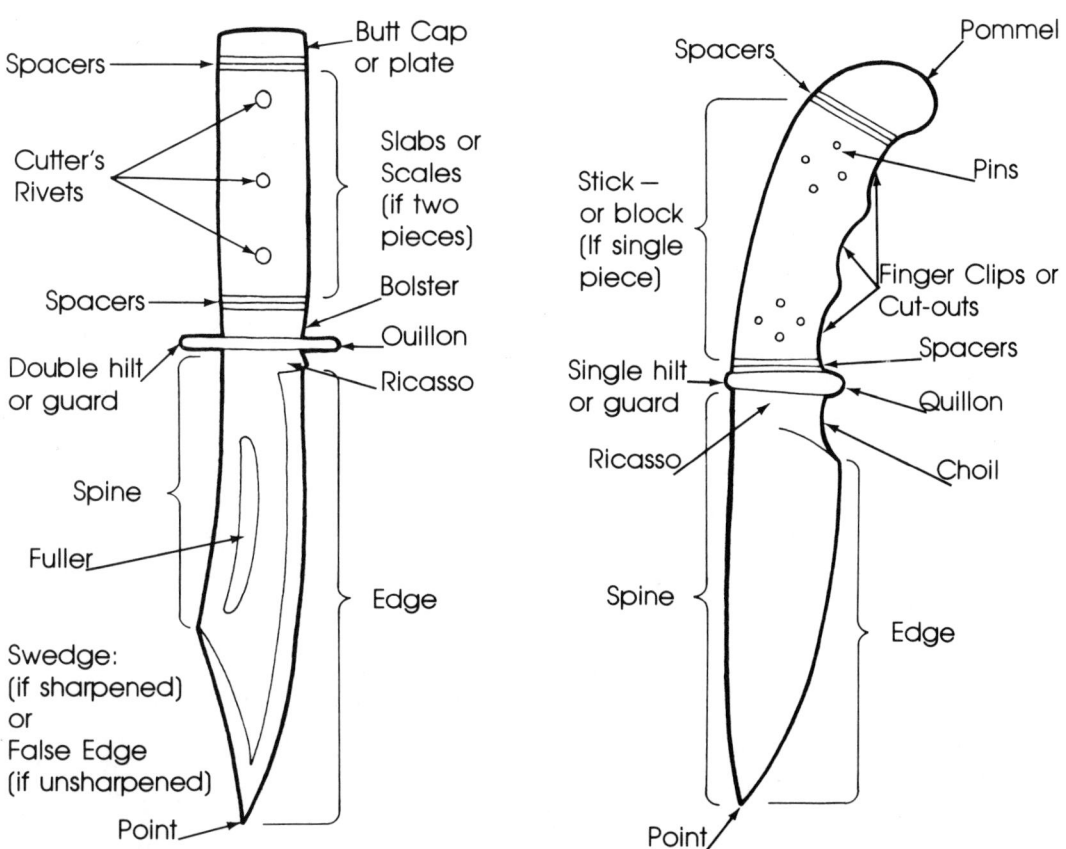

Today, most hunting and fishing knives have one quillon, and most fighting knives have two. It's a logical arrangement, and one you want to keep in mind when designing your knife.

Glancing at the accompanying illustrations, you'll note that the back, or non-cutting edge, of single-edged knives is called the *spine*. Daggers and other double-edged knives also have spines, but in their case the spine runs down the center of the blade. Using this as our guide, we can agree that the spine by definition is the thickest portion of the blade viewed in cross section.

For added rigidity, some of today's knives have gone to ridiculously thick spines—from 1/4-inch up to 5/16-inch in some instances. The problem here is that spines of this thickness add to the weight of the knife making it more difficult to slice or skin with.

A far more useful (and thankfully more common) spine thickness is from 1/8-inch to 3/16-inch. I cannot imagine a modern-day use for which a 3/16-inch spine would not be adequate, and for most purposes the narrower (1/8-inch) width will suffice. Some special purpose knives, notably those designed for filleting, have spines that are only a hair over 1/16-inch in width. The objective here, of course, is to produce a highly flexible blade that will follow contours of the object being cut, i.e. the fish's backbone. There's a lot to be said for caping blades with some flexibility.

That portion of the blade, across the back, that runs from the point of the knife up to the spine is known as the *swedge* if it is sharpened, and the *false edge* if it is not sharpened. Most fighting knives, including the famous Bowie, are swedged. Most hunting knives, with the exception of special-purpose skinners, are not. Some knowledgeable outdoorsmen like to do their skinning with a blade that is swedged (i.e. sharpened) for about 3/8-inch to 1/2-inch above the point. Swedging any blade is an easy task for the home hobbyist.

The cutting portion of the blade is called the *edge*. It follows logically that fighting knives that are sharpened on both edges are referred to as being double-edged, while those sharpened on only one edge are known as single-edged. A swedged blade is still single-edged, no matter how far back from the point the swedge extends.

On some blades, but by no means all, you will observe a thickened, unsharpened portion immediately below the hilt. This is known as the *ricasso*, and on sheath knives it serves two functions. First, it extends the strength of the tang into the blade, and second, it allows the cutting edge to be sharpened throughout its entire length without difficulty. Ricassos are necessary to the functioning of folding knives, but on sheath knives they are optional.

On some knives you also will note that a portion of the blade immediately below the hilt, on the cutting edge, is cut out or concave. This configuration is referred to as the *choil* or finger clip. Choils are intended primarily to give better blade control (as during a difficult skinning or caping job) by allowing the index finger to be extended over the hilt and wrapped around the upper portion of the blade. Choils also improve on the function of the ricasso in allowing easy sharpening of the full length of the cutting edge. Seldom seen on hunting knives and skinners a few years ago, choils are increasingly popular and now are found on many fine blades.

As alluded to earlier, the portion of the knife that you hold in your hand is the *handle* or *grip*. We will discuss in considerable depth later on that the handle can be constructed of almost any material which suits your fancy. Hardwoods, Micarta, leather, and stag are the materials best suited and most commonly used.

That part of the knife that extends through the handle, either partially or all the way, is known as the *tang*. The tang is essentially an extension of the blade, except that it is usually *annealed* rather than *hardened*. If the handle completely encloses the tang, the tang will be of round, modified, or short design, and the handle is known as a *block* or *stick*. If the tang is exposed and follows the general outline of the handle, the tang is of *full* design, and the wood or other material affixed to it are known as *scales or* slabs.

Most handles being made today are contoured to fit the user's hand, and many have cutouts that help position the user's fingers. These cutouts are sometimes called finger *clips.* When the handle is designed with a single finger cutout for the index finger, it is sometimes called a choil, although this designation seems a trifle confusing.

The butt or upper portion of the handle may feature a shaped piece of metal, stag or other material that is known as a *pommel* or *butt cap.* Although the terms are frequently used interchangeably, I prefer to distinguish between them by using the term pommel if it swells or protrudes beyond the contour of the grip, and butt cap if it continues the same general contour of the grip. I further distinguish between butt cap and *butt plate,* by using the latter term if the piece is 1/4-inch or less in thickness.

*Italicized words are defined in the glossary.

CHAPTER 3

UNDERSTANDING METALLURGY:
The Steel-Maker's Art

I can't promise you that a nodding acquaintance with metallurgy will help you become more proficient as a knife-maker. I can promise you, though, that it will add to your enjoyment of the art and maybe even impress your friends.

Literally thousands of different steels have been formulated over the years by engineers and metallurgists looking for just the right properties to perform specialized jobs. Making a knife blade is about as specialized an assignment as you can think of and any number of steels have been put to this use.

Don't let anyone tell you that any single steel will satisfy your knife-making requirement. It just ain't so. But just about everyone develops his own favorites as he goes along and likely you will too.

All that I will say about metals is this book will be directed at knife-making. But to understand what makes a good knife steel, we're going to have to touch on some developments not directly related to our primary interest.

To begin, there are four broad types or classifications of commercially useful steels: carbon, alloy, high-alloy, and tool. To these, space age technology has added a fifth type of material in which other elements—nickel, cobalt, molybdenum, and others—have replaced iron to the extent that it's hardly correct to call it steel anymore. For lack of a better word, the term super-alloy is usually used. It's importance to knife-making is limited but interesting.

Steels Used in Knife-making

Nearly all modern knife-making steels of consequence can be classified as *alloy, high-alloy,* or *tool.* The latter type still predominates, but some of the high-alloy metals are moving up fast among custom knife-makers.

The terms *high-carbon* and *tool* steel are often used synonymously, but this interchanging is not precisely correct because tool steels in use today run the gamut from simple carbon compounds (in which no alloying element is used) to alloys containing several different elements in addition to carbon.

As used today, the *carbon steel* classification is applied to all plain (non-alloy) steels in commercial use. The amount of carbon used controls the response of a steel to hardening treatments. Thus, when we speak of a high-carbon steel, we're talking about the harder steels. By definition, low-carbon steel contains from .02 to .30 percent carbon, medium-carbon steel contains from .30 to .60 percent carbon, and high-carbon steel contains more than .60 percent carbon and may range as high as 1.7 percent.

Simple alloy steels (which is what most of today's tool steels are) have a relatively high carbon content (usually about 1.0 percent), and also contain moderate amounts of chromium, tungsten, and molybdenum.

Steels are classified as high-alloy when the level of alloys added to them exceeds 10 percent. Each alloy used in steel has its own special purpose. Chromium improves hardness and resists corrosion; nickel increases toughness and resistance to heat and acids; manganese improves strength and resistance to wear; molybdenum increases strength and resistance to heat; tungsten retains hardness at high temperatures; and vanadium increases strength and ductility.

Stainless steel is a high-alloy material with special ability to resist corrosion, a property obtained primarily through the addition of chromium. Nickel also is used in fairly substantial quantities in some stainless steels, a fact that has led to a secondary classification of these steels as chromium or nickel-chromium. About 30 different types of stainless steel are in fairly common usage today, and two in particular—440C and 154CM—are particularly popular as knife-making material.

This large drop-point hunter was built around one of the superlative "Dale's Blades" from Indian Ridge Traders. The author considers this line of blades, factory ground from 440C stainless steel, to be among the finest available to American knife-makers. He used ivory Micarta for the handle and brass bar stock for the hilt and butt cap.

Alpha-Numeric Designations

Since I've introduced the thought, this seems as good a time as any to discuss all those alphabetic and numeric designations that you're sure to hear tossed around by fellow knife-makers. I'm not sure that all of them know what they're talking about, but let's make sure that you do.

Back around the turn of the century, the proliferating types and grades of steel being developed and used was already becoming a problem and a nuisance. Then, as now, many steels were being given names by sales departments that had little to do with their real properties and characteristics.

Taking note of the growing confusion, the Society of Automotive Engineers (SAE) issued in 1912 a group of compositional limits for steels to be used in making automobiles. Each classification was assigned a number, and each specification within that classification was identified by its own particular alpha-numeric codification. These SAE steels were gradually increased over the years, and their compositional limits were kept in good working order by periodic revisions.

For a number of years now, the American Iron and Steel Institute (AISI) has collaborated with the SAE in publishing this continuously updated list used to control the chemical analyses of steels. Many of the steels included in today's list were developed for purposes other than for automobile manufacture, hence the same basic system has been found flexible enough to accommodate all newcomers.

Other standards and codification systems, notably those developed by the American Society for Testing and Materials (ASTM) and the American Society of Mechanical Engineers (ASME) also are used today, but these are intended for more specialized purposes, and are of marginal interest to knife-makers.

By referring to the AISI-SAE classification system, we find that steel specified as 440C is a chromium stainless having the following compositional limits:

Element	Percent Alloyed
Carbon	1.00
Chromium	17.05
Manganese	.50
Molybdenum	.45
Nickel	.20
Silicon	.40

Adding up the total of these alloying elements, we find that 19.60 percent of 440C stainless steel is composed of elements other than iron. Looking back at our previous definition of what constitutes high-alloy steel (more than 10 percent alloys), we find that 440C fits the bill.

The other stainless (high-alloy) steel I mentioned as having some popularity among knife-makers is 154CM. According to its AISI-SAE codification, this is a high-chromium (14.00 percent), high-molybdenum (4.00 percent) steel. As we noted earlier, molybdenum is added to steel to improve its strength and resistance to heat. This fits, because 154CM was originally developed for use in superspeed jet airplanes. America's custom knife-makers, who are constantly experimenting, soon found that it also has some properties which make it a superior knife-building material.

Several of the other steels that are popular for knife-making were developed as tool steels, although their composition may also qualify them as high-alloy steels. One such steel is D2, which is classified as a high-carbon, high-chromium tool steel. Its carbon content is 1.50 percent and its chromium content is 11.50 percent. It also contains 1.00 percent molybdenum and .90 percent vanadium. Another popular knife-making steel is F8, which is a carbon-tungsten steel containing 8.00 percent tungsten and 4.00 percent chromium. Although not considered a true "stainless" steel, it has a high resistance to corrosion.

The AISI-SAE classification system for tool steels, in addition to setting compositional limits, also groups steels according to usage and hardening characteristics. In the latter category are the oil-hardening, water-hardening, and air-hardening

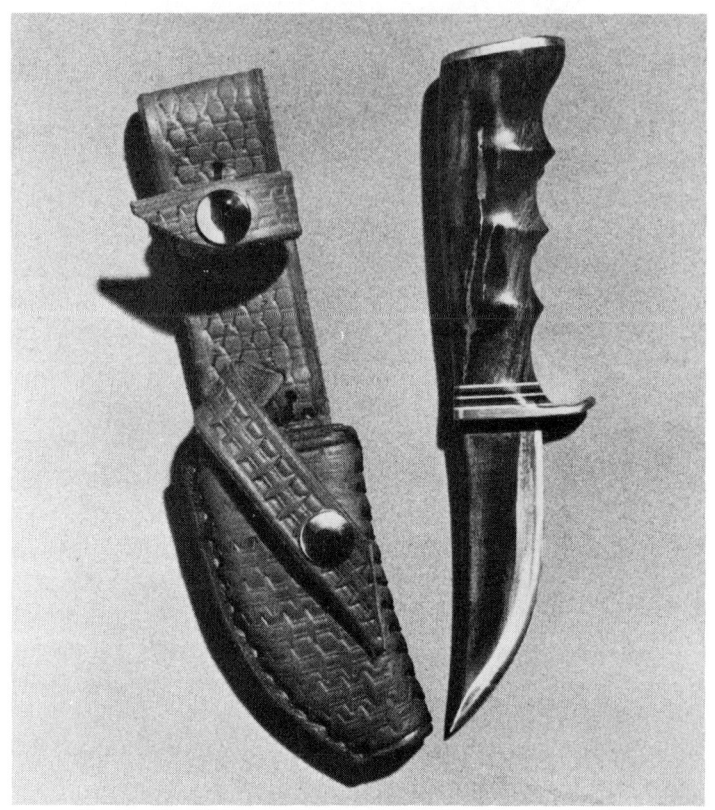

This small game skinner and hunter was made by home hobbyist P. W. (Phil) Timm of Butte, Montana. Blade is ground from molybdenum steel tempered to a Rockwell hardness of 60-62, and handle is of phenol-impregnated Arizona ironwood. Sheath is of heavy cowhide with hardwood liner. Timm is typical of those hobbyists who began knife-making as a hobby, and then began selling knives to a limited clientele. (Photo courtesy Dick Blasius, president, Indian Ridge Traders.)

steels. Usage classifications include such characteristics as high-speed (for example, drillbits) and shock-resisting steels.

Among the more popular knife steels classified in this manner are A2 (an air-hardening steel), O1 (An oil-hardening steel), and W2 (a water-hardening steel). We'll take a closer look at hardening properties when we get to the chapter on heat-treating.

High-speed (molybdenum and tungsten base) tool steels also have found some application in the knife-maker's craft, though for my money they are too brittle for knife blades. Of these, a molybdenum base tool steel known as M2 is probably the most popular at present.

PROPERTIES OF GOOD KNIFE STEEL

There are several properties that are sought in a good knife blade. At the top of my list I would place *hardness* (though not excessively hard), *toughness, ductility, elasticity,* and *corrosion resistance.* Elasticity is important primarily in filleting knives, and if I had to leave another property off my list, it would be corrosion resistance. (That's why the Good Lord made WD-40.)

To some extent, these desirable characteristics tend to work against one another, and it is the search for an optimum combination that keeps knife-makers looking for something better.

I won't quibble with those who seem to think otherwise, but hardness is related—very directly in my experience—to a blade's ability to hold its cutting edge. The problem, of course, is that excessive hardness makes it hard as blazes to sharpen your blade, and it also equates with brittleness. Toughness is the property that is exactly opposite to brittleness, and that's why I place it second in importance to hardness. What you have to look for is a good trade-off between these two important properties. Ductility is important too, because it relates to the blade's ability to be deformed or distorted without breaking.

THE ROCKWELL TEST

Because of the importance of hardness in the steel-making process, no fewer than six tests have been developed to measure this property (and there may be more I haven't heard about yet). The *Rockwell test* is the one most often applied to knife steel, and the one you'll see quoted most often by the knife-makers' supply houses.

The Rockwell testing device has two different scales—a "B" scale that's used to test soft metals (indentation is produced by a hard steel ball), and the "C" scale used to test steel and other hard metals (indentation is produced by a diamond cone under a load of 150 kilograms). For those like me who have long since forgotten their metric tables, that figures out to about 330.69 pounds. I think.

The shorthand expression for hardness measured on the Rockwell "C" scale is commonly written OO-Rc, though I've seen it expressed in at least a half dozen other ways as well. As long as the subject is knife blades, it doesn't really matter, because it's the only test used, 100 times out of 100.

The metal's resistance to indentation is read directly on a scale on the testing device that registers from -3 to +68. Harder metals, such as those used for knife blades, register on the upper end of the scale.

Most knife-makers, and I include myself, like a hardness of about 57-Rc—give or take a point—because it offers a reasonable trade-off between edge-holding ability and ease of sharpening. The highly alloyed stainless steels, such as 440C and 154CM, run a tad higher, say around 60-Rc, and sure enough, they're harder to sharpen. I've never worked with the previously mentioned D2, but I'm told it's as hard as a landlord's heart.

There are a couple of anomalies we should mention in passing, if for no other reason than to preclude your having to say "nobody ever told me that."

With some of today's special purpose steels, hardness doesn't necessarily equate with edge-holding ability. Some of the high-alloy and superalloy steels that have been developed in recent years shoot the needle right off the old Rockwell scale. Yet they won't hold an edge worth sour apples. Happily for us home hobbyists, others have already experimented with these metals and found them wanting. So you don't have to worry about them turning up in a blade or piece of stock you order from any reputable supplier.

The other material that deserves mention is a nonferrous sintered material known as Stellite 6K. Some of the custom knife-makers are fooling around with it, and it will probably be turning up in the supply house catalogues if it hasn't already.

Sintered alloy, should you be unfamiliar with the term, is sort of a conglomerate of powdered elements fused together under extreme pressure but at temperatures below the melting point of most of its constituents. Because gun-makers have used it to some extent, I happen to be familiar with it.

Stellite 6K derives its hardness from carbide particles that are suspended in the mixture. It registers only about 45-Rc, but it's so hard that a knife blade made from it must be sharpened with a diamond-surfaced lapping tool rather than a good old Arkansas oilstone.

STEELS FROM SHEFFIELD AND SOLINGEN

We've already mentioned that the English and German cities of Sheffield and Solingen held a special place in the hearts of knife enthusiasts. And for good reason! They've been in the cutlery business since before this country was discovered. But some suppliers seem to trade on these names as though they possessed some special sort of magic, and tend to imply that any blade from either place is bound to be a good 'un.

Lots of blades being made in Sheffield and Solingen *are* good—no question about it. But the designation—of itself—means no more than specifying that a piece of knife steel originates in Pittsburgh, Gary, or' East Chicago. It's the *steel* that counts, not the city of origin.

Having said this, I want to go on and mention that blades made in Sheffield in particular, represent a strange admix of 18th century tradition and 20th century technology. The better Sheffield blades are shaped individually by masters who have been in the business for years. To obtain the same quality from a U.S. maker, you will have to go to one of the custom-makers and pay several times more.

I've been told by people whose opinions I respect that experts can identify the products of individual Sheffield blade grinders, because each is marked with its own subtle variations.

Even in England, where traditions are cherished, the old ways are dying out, and hand-ground Sheffield blades are always in short supply. Indian Ridge Traders, listed in the appendix, is one of the more reputable sources in this country, and, the last time I checked, Atlanta Cutlery still offered some excellent Solingen blades. E. Christopher Firearms Company is the exclusive U.S. distributor for a leading line of Solingen blades. Many you buy elsewhere come through them.

CHAPTER 4

SETTING UP YOUR WORKBENCH

Nearly every home workshop already contains the essential tools you will need for knife-making. I've never tried it, but I suppose it might be possible to put together some sort of a knife on the kitchen table. (But don't you ever tell the little woman that Uncle Jim suggested it.)

By my definition, however, anyone who calls himself a *home hobbyist* (a sobriquet I regard as somewhat akin to the Legion of Merit and Congressional Medal of Honor rolled into one) is going to have a sturdy workbench overhung by a pegboard for assorted hand tools. For the purposes of our discussion, at least, we're going to assume that such is the case.

Strange as it may seem, one of the handiest tools you have for making a good, sharp knife is ... a good, sharp knife. Don't ask me how the first knife-maker did his thing; it's one of those imponderables better left to philosophers and such. You'll use your knife (the one you already have) for cutting leather for the sheath, shaping the handle, and a dozen and one other jobs that will suggest themselves as you go along.

You'll also need three types of saws: A hacksaw for cutting soft metal used in both the pommel and guard; a backsaw for cutting slabs, antlers, and other handle material; and a coping or jigsaw for shaping the handle material, making finger clips, and the like.

Files are next on our list. You can get by with a flat or mill file of ordinary persuasion, a round or rattail file for shaping the hilt, a rasp for shaping the handle, and a few needle files for slotting the guard and sundry other tasks that larger files can't reach. Many hardware stores don't carry needle files, so try a local hobby-supply store. X-Acto, among others, packages a set of six files with a handle that sells for about $7.50 in my area.

If you don't already have a ball peen hammer or two, you should invest in one. I have several, but find that I use the 12-oz size most often. A tack hammer is too light, and a carpenter's hammer has too large a head for knife-making chores; best buy a ball peen hammer and tell the wife it's for fixing the washing machine.

Typical of many home workshops, though possibly with a few more special-purpose tools than most, this workbench was designed by the author to provide ready accessibility for most of his tools. Note bench-mounted hand drill at left end of the workbench.

Handtools used by author in his knife-making activities include, from left, ball peen hammers, flexible shaft with rotary rasp, assortment of files and rasps, rotary sanding discs, buffers, and polishers, rotary rasp assortment, soft Arkansas oilstone, propane torch with silver solder, Dremel Moto-Tool, variable-speed hand drill, and a selection of saws (coping, back, and hacksaw).

Nearly every workbench has a vise, and vises are absolutely essential for knife-making. I can't decide whether I use the carpenter's or the mechanic's vise the most, and I've got to admit it's pretty much a toss-up. The first you'll use for holding the handle as you shape it, and the latter you'll use for holding the blade as you solder the hilt, drill the tang, and shape both hilt and pommel. If you do not have either vise, and it's an either/or decision, I'd lean to the mechanic's vise. You can use wood blocks to protect your handle as you shape it, and you really do need steel jaws for soldering, bending tangs, and such.

You're obviously going to need sharpening stones. Most workbenches have a Carborundum stone or two, but for knife-making you need a soft Arkansas oilstone as well. A hard surgical stone is nice but unnecessary.

A good light that you can direct on your work is another mighty helpful item. The best, of course, are the specially made workbench lamps with adjustable arms. But you can rig up your own from an old desk lamp or simply a shaded bulb. The idea is to have something you can throw directly on your work when you're doing some of the more tedious but necessary chores.

About the only other non-powered tool you absolutely have to have is a good propane torch. You'll use it for joining hilt to tang with silver solder and for heating metal so you can bend it. A conventional soldering iron or electric gun simply won't produce enough heat for knife-making purposes.

CHEATING WITH THE HAND DRILL

Now we come to the one powered tool that I consider indispensable for knife-making. It's the variable-speed hand drill with 3/8-inch chuck. How the modern home handyman manages to keep home and hearth together without one, I'll never know. And for knife-making, unless you're looking for a full-time occupation instead of a hobby, it's a necessity.

If we started counting on our fingers the different uses of a hand drill for knife-making, we'd likely run out of fingers before we did uses. It's obviously a drill, but it's also a sander, a buffer, a polisher, and a router.

For the hand drill to attain its ultimate usefulness, some improvisation is needed. First thing you've got to do is secure it to your workbench, and for this purpose a simple bench mount can be made from scrap material you have lying around.

The accompanying illustration shows how to assemble your bench mount. The best construction material I've found is the particle board used to make shelving. It's better than one-inch wood because it won't split, and it's easier to work with than ¾-inch plywood.

The hand drill is held in place by a ½-inch metal strap like they use for clothes dryer vent pipes. The slots at the top of the two upright end pieces are lined with foam rubber weather stripping. That's all there is to it.

With your hand drill mounted securely, the accessories you'll need to fully equip it are available at most hardware stores. These include a good selection of high-speed bits, a 4-inch diameter medium-grit grinding wheel, two or three 6-inch buffing wheels (one for each buffing-compound grit that you use), one or two sanding discs in either 4-inch or 6-inch diameters, a modest assortment of rotary rasps, and a cutting point for inletting handle scales.

One item that will add immeasurably to your drill's versatility is a flexible shaft. Some hardware stores carry them, or you can order one from Coastal Abrasive and Tool Co., Trumbull CT 06611.

Here let me mention one small caveat that can cost you the price of a new hand drill if you ignore it. Don't try to use a heavy standary-duty

The schematic drawing shows how to make a simple bench mount that vastly increases the versatility of the variable-speed, 3/8-inch hand drill. Materials and construction technique are described in text.

Homemade Bench Mount for Hand Drill

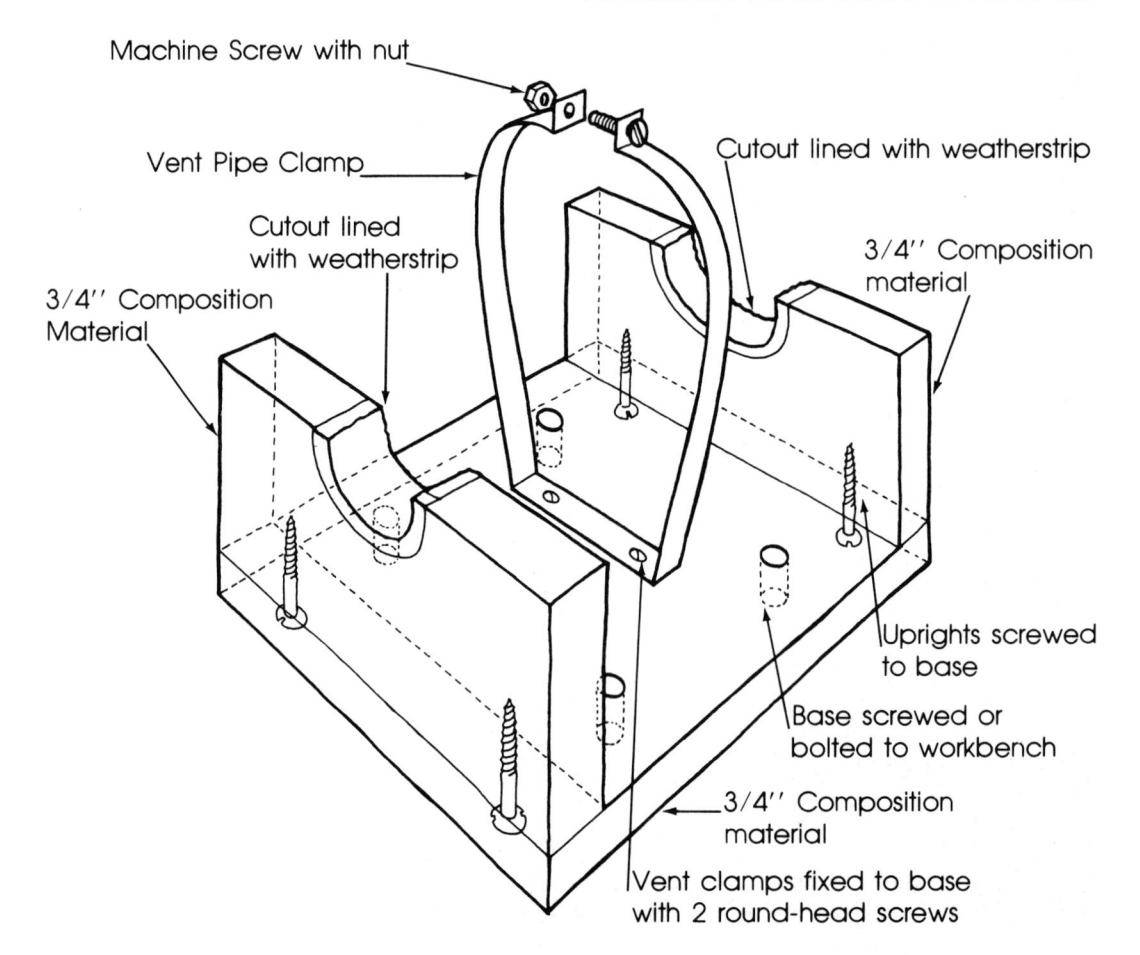

grinding wheel on your drill. The bearings of the drill simply can't take that much weight, and besides being dangerous, you'll burn out your drill in short order. Don't use a grinding wheel that is more than 4 inches in diameter or more than ½-inch thick.

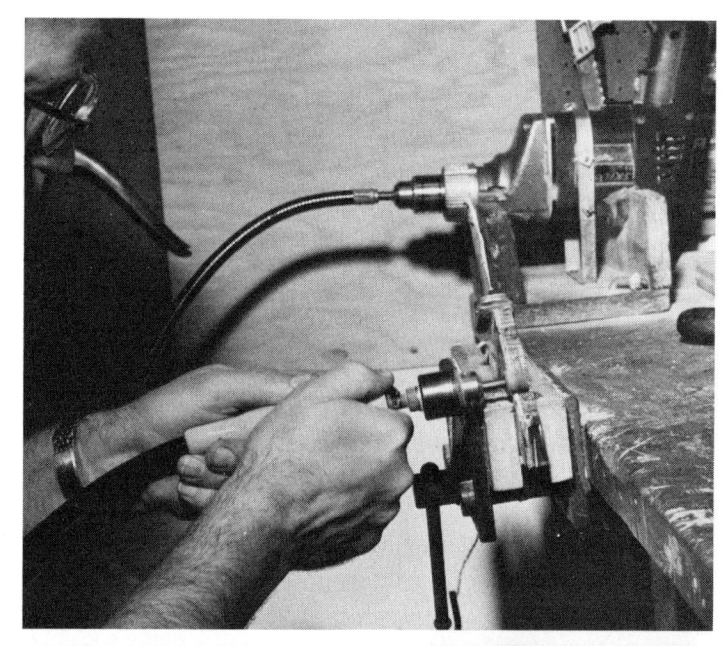

A flexible shaft, such as this one available from Coastal Abrasive and Tool Co, gives the home hobbyist greater flexibility in his use of the bench-mounted hand drill. Shaft is used with drum sanders and rotary files and rasps for a variety of knife-making chores.

Fitted with arbor and dressed with red or brown rouge, muslin buffing wheels chucked in bench-mounted hand drill do yeoman duty for putting a satin finish on knife blades. Mirror finish requires felt wheel dressed with white rouge. The variable-speed drill is also ideal for grinding when fitted with 4-inch diameter wheel.

Buffing wheels are substantially lighter, and the 6-inch diameters are fine. You can get dandy little 4-inch buffing wheels from the Kirby Company (yep, the vacuum cleaner people). Kirby also carries stick-type red rouge that stays on the wheel better than most. Kirby's grinding and buffing wheels have a special triangular shaft that won't chuck in a ½-inch drill. But they work fine in a ⅜-inch chuck.

OTHER NICE-TO-HAVE POWER TOOLS

There are obviously some other power tools that will speed up your knife-making. If you already have them, fine, but they aren't absolutely necessary.

At the top of my nice-to-have list I'd put a bench grinder. These operate at much higher RPM than do hand drills, and thus make grinding and buffing operations go a good deal faster. I've got one, and a fair number of the illustrations in this book show me using it. But remember, anything you can do on a bench grinder, you can do with a bench mounted hand drill.

A drill press is another nice but not really necessary power tool for knife-making. I made a bunch of knives before I got one, and I still don't use it all that much for knife-making. If you have one, use it for drilling the parallel holes in handle blocks. If you don't have one, a little patience and a reasonably steady hand will let you do the job just as well with a hand drill.

Professional knife-makers have all sorts of powered equipment that they use, including bench mounted belt sanders, metal-cutting band-saws, and specialized buffers. One of the big reasons I decided to write this book was because every other book I read on the subject kept talking about the professionals using this stuff. Sure I'd like to have it, but for me—and I assume you—knife-making is strictly a hobby. I plan to keep it that way, and hundreds of dollars worth of special equipment just don't fit into my budget.

There is one more little gadget that I've found

to be the cat's meow for all sorts of workbench chores including, of course, knife-making. I speak of the Dremel Moto-Tool, made by a division of Emerson Electric in Racine, Wisconsin. Most hobby shops stock them.

These little cuties are ridiculously expensive (my opinion, not theirs) and sound like a mad dentist on the loose. But they'll do just about everything except make coffee.

Should you decide to invest in a Moto-Tool, take your Uncle Jim's advice and get a model with ball bearings rather than brass bushings. Those of you who suffered through the brass-bushing era of spinning reels know whereof I speak. Dremel's Model 381, which also offers variable speeds from 5,000 to 25,000 RPM, is their top of the line. You can own one for around the 70 bucks you're going to save by making your own custom-designed knife. (Well, my wife uses that kind of logic, so why shouldn't I?)

Even if the price of a Moto-Tool is too rich for your blood, drop around to your local hobby shop and pick up a couple of Dremel's tungsten carbide cutting tips. They work nearly as well in a hand drill (especially if you equip it with a flexible shaft).

The Dremel Moto-Tool, shown here being used to cut tang slot in spacer material, is useful for a variety of knife-making chores. The author advises the purchase of a variable-speed model with ball bearings for long life and satisfactory service.

MAKE YOUR SHOP A SAFE ONE

It's always a temptation to assume that everyone knows and practices good workshop safety. Unfortunately, statistics tell us otherwise. Knife-making is no different from anything else that requires the use of tools that burn and cut. Use 'em wrong and you'll get hurt.

Here are some basic safety rules that I hope you'll try to follow. All of them are nothing more than common sense, but that's the basis of the best safety rules I know:

1. During all your operations, wrap the blade of your knife in several thicknesses of masking

One of the more basic safety rules of knife-making is to wrap blade in several layers of masking tape. Tape should be removed only during grinding, buffing, and soldering operations.

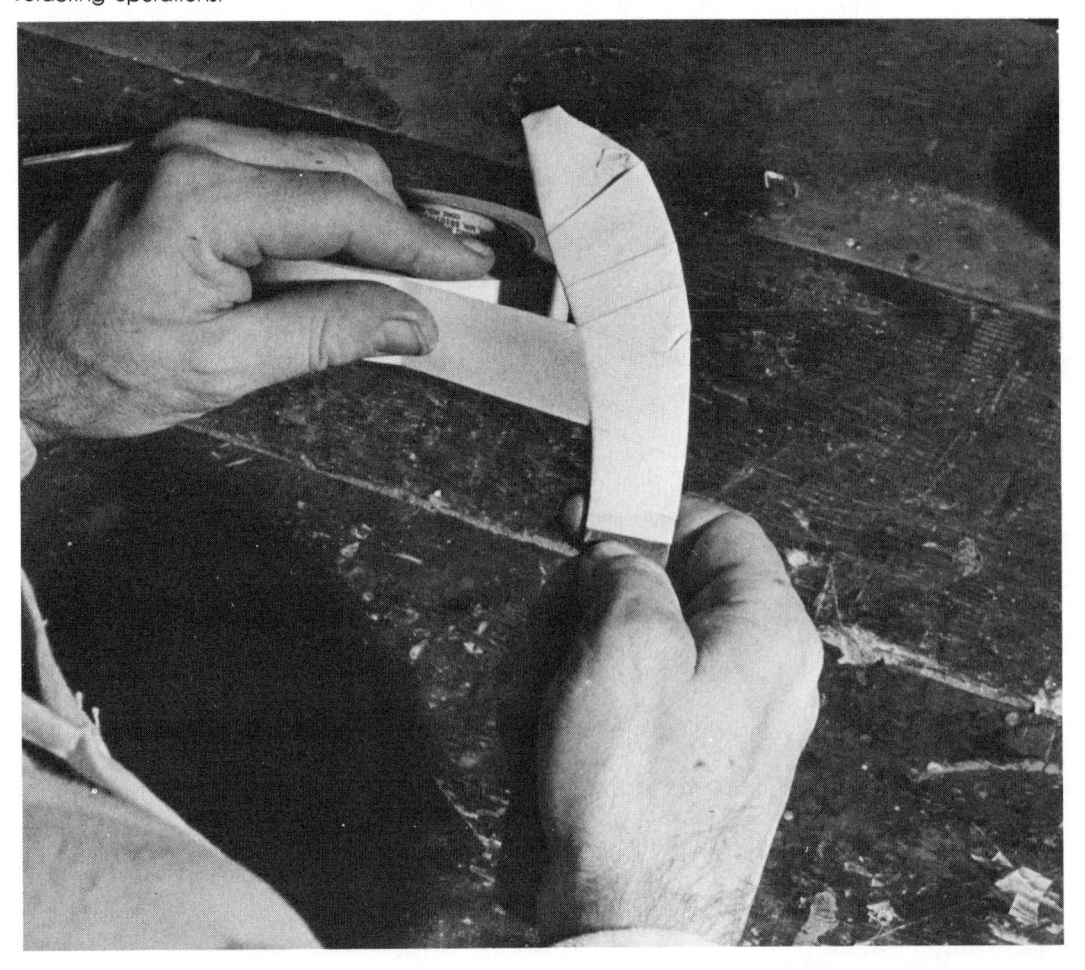

tape to protect both it and you. Check the tape from time to time, and replace it when it becomes worn.

2. When soldering or using a torch for any reason, be sure that all flammable objects are well removed from the vicinity of the flame. Use a steel vise to hold objects being headed, and make certain the vise itself is free of oil and solvents.

3. Use the safety shields provided with bench grinders, and **wear safety glasses when working with any power tool.** If you wear prescription glasses, be sure they are ground from plastic or tempered glass. If you don't regularly wear eyeglasses, use safety glasses.

4. Don't wear loose-fitting clothing when working with flames or powered equipment. A shop apron made of heavy denim is a good investment.

5. When sawing, filing, or sharpening, be sure the object you are working with is clamped in a vise or to the workbench. Two-hand control is one of the best safety rules you can have.

6. Keep your work area free of clutter and keep flammables off the workbench when not in use. Have a place for every tool, and keep every tool in its place.

7. Work bare-handed. Any little nicks or burns that gloves may save your fingers are more than offset by their propensity for getting wrapped around power tools. Gloves may be justified when working with a torch, but other times they are bad medicine.

CHAPTER 5

GETTING STARTED: Where There's a Will, There's a Knife

In my youth (and actually well beyond), handmade knives were ground from old files, cut from circular saw blades, fashioned from car springs, or otherwise made from whatever metal seemed handy at the time.

For a period in my early teens, I was the envy of every kid in the little Texas town where I grew up, because my dad owned an auto-repair shop. The shop had the usual assortment of grinding wheels and other metal-working tools, and I spent many a pleasant Saturday afternoon grinding away at some obscure piece of metal that I hoped would eventually resemble a knife.

Back in those pleasurable days, when single-action Colts sold for $12 and every pawnshop had 'em by the score, we still had blacksmiths who could build practically anything from metal. I became acquainted with several of these worthy souls because my family kept horses.

On days when I wasn't hunting, fishing, or happily grinding away, I could usually be found peering over the shoulder of a delightful old gentleman named Jason Jackson. Mr. Jackson was one of the few smithies willing to tolerate my presence, and it was from him I learned the rudiments of metalworking. It was also to him that I went when the problems of hardening or tempering a ground blade taxed my inconsequential knowledge of the mysterious art of knife-making.

Few of the knives I made in those years were worthy of the name, and fewer still survived my adolescent penchant for knife-throwing and swapping. But I made them, and to me they were things of beauty and grace. Strangely enough, judged against the store-bought competition of that Depression era, they probably weren't all that bad.

In those days anyone who would lay down more than $1.98 for a knife—be it a folder or hunter—was summarily judged a candidate for the funny farm. And why not—.22 cartridges were 30 cents per box and good shotguns regularly changed hands for only $20.

For better or for worse (I leave that judgment to you), those days belong to the past. No longer is it necessary (though it can still be fun) to scrounge back alleys and junk piles for knife-making material. Nowadays, thanks to the tremendous interest in knife collecting and making, there are a number of reputable firms whose reason for being is to sell you beautifully ground and polished blades and other parts that await only your artistic touch to convert them to hunting pals or arty wall hangers.

DEALING WITH SUPPLY HOUSES

Most of the knife-making supply houses in business today exist because their proprietors have an abiding interest in fine cutlery. Some have grown up around gun-supply houses, possibly because knife-makers and gunsmiths often use tools of common calling.

Several of the better knife-making supply houses are one-man or one-family enterprises, and their catalogs and specification sheets are often more utilitarian than artistic. By and large, they are friendly folk, given to first names and helpful information. Some sell only limited lines of blades or accessory equipment, while others inventory dozens of different lines, including imports, and specialized power tools with price tags that run into the hundreds of dollars.

Rather than attempt to list the supply houses here, I've mentioned some of their names with reference to special items (such as buffing compound) covered elsewhere in the book. I've also included in the appendix, a list of suppliers I've dealt with over the past few years.

Getting started right involves little more than sitting down and writing letters to four or five of the supply houses. Most of them will ask that you include 50 cents or a dollar to cover handling costs. I've asked a couple of suppliers about this charge, and they make the point that only about one inquiry in 10 results in a follow-up order. I can see their point.

Also, because many of these suppliers are one-man operations (often with mama acting as secretary), don't expect any miracles of speediness. You may wait a month or so before your letter brings a response. (Fortunately, most of them seem to respond to actual orders more rapidly than they do requests for literature.) It does get a little frustrating when you're raring to go, but I don't know any cure for it.

DECIDING ON THE KNIFE YOU WANT

Once you have three or four supply-house catalogs in hand, you're ready for the next step: Deciding on the type, shape, and size of the knife or knives you want to make. This subject is discussed more fully in later chapters, but generally what you want to do is make an initial decision on whether you want a working knife or a wall

STRAIGHT HUNTER

CLIP POINT HUNTER

DROP-POINT HUNTER

BOWIE

PUSH KNIFE

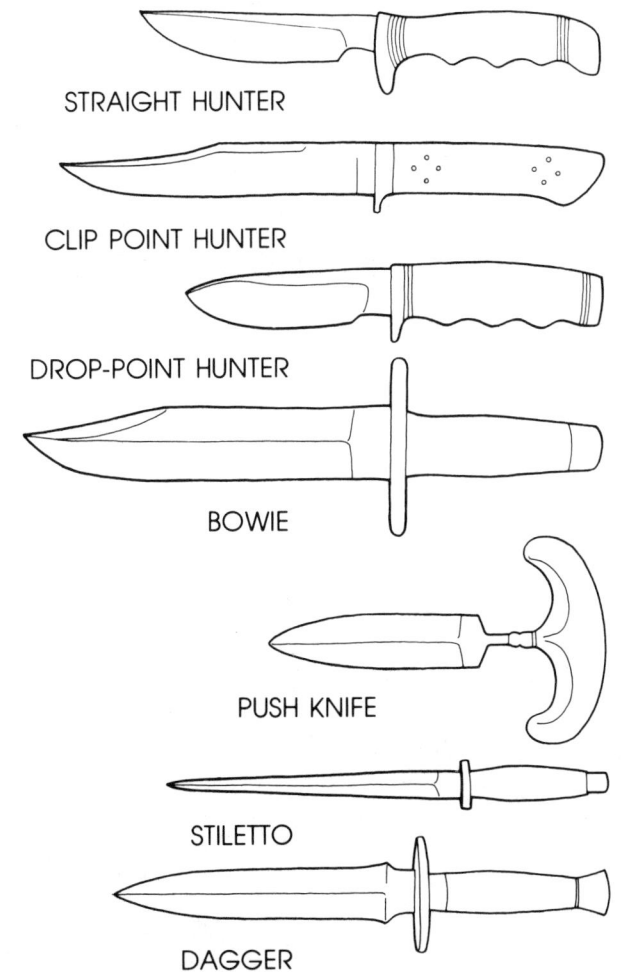

STILETTO

DAGGER

More than a score of supply houses now stock tools, parts, and accessories used by both amateur and professional knife-makers. Many of their catalogs, in addition to providing the home hobbyist easy accessibility to blades, blanks, handle and spacer materials, and cast and bar stock for hilts and pommels, are veritable treasure troves of practical ideas for knife-making.

TYPICAL KNIFE DESIGNS

After centuries of evolution, the knife designs illustrated here have endured as perennial favorites. Of the seven basic designs shown, only the push knife, stiletto, and dagger serve little practical purpose in today's society and are therefore generally considered "wall hangers" of primary interest to collectors.

hanger, a skinning or general-purpose blade, a drop-point or a straight blade, a hunting knife or a fishing blade that doubles for filleting chores.

If it's a working knife you're after, how much will you use it and under what conditions? Is your game mostly whitetails, or do you plan on going after an elk this year? Are you strictly a meat

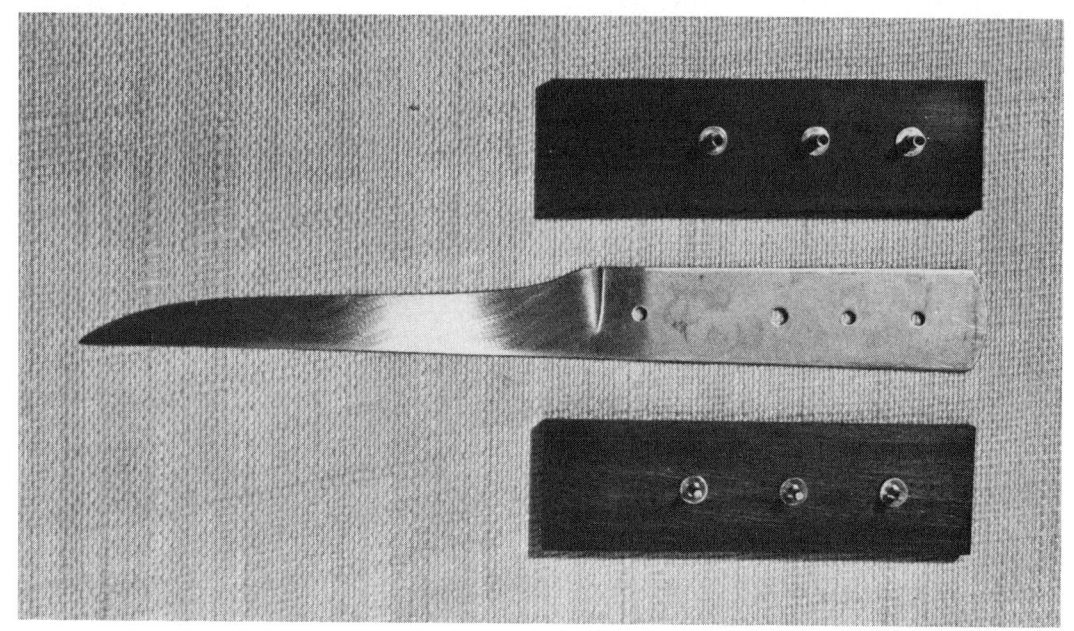

Planning the design of your knife involves ordering and laying out the component parts that will go into its construction. Whether it's a simple full-tang filleting knife (above), or a more complicated hunter (right) the process is the same.

hunter, or do you plan to cape your trophy? If fishing is your game, will stainless steel serve you better than a carbon steel blade?

These are decisions that only you can make. But they are important ones. The best advice I can give you—besides, of course, reading this book all the way through—is to study the catalogs carefully *before* you order your supplies.

With the crucial choice of blade behind you, give some thought to how you want the rest of your knife to look. The shape and size of the blade, and its intended purpose will influence your decision heavily. You probably won't want a double-hilt on a knife you plan to use primarily for skinning. Nor is stag or leather the best handle material for a knife you plan to throw in your tackle box.

Which of the soft metals—brass, aluminum, or nickel-silver—do you prefer for hilt and pommel? Each has its own advantages and disadvantages, as we shall see in the chapter dealing with these topics. Or perhaps you have in mind a knife in which handle and hilt are integral and pommel is omitted. It's not a bad design for a fishing or bird knife.

At this point, I think you'll find it helpful to sit down with graph paper and pencil and sketch the knife you have in mind. Do a little experimenting (paper is cheap) and develop what you consider to be the ideal blade and handle for your purpose. Legend has it that Jim Bowie carved from soft pine a model of the knife he made famous. It's not all that bad an idea!

MAKING DO WITH WHAT YOU HAVE

Now you have it all together. You've decided which blade(s) to order; you know the configuration of the knife you want to make; you've developed some pretty definite ideas on what handle material you would prefer to use.

The next thing to do is look around the house and workshop and see what you have in hand that might look better made into a knife. I've made some pretty nifty hilts, for example, from the cranks of broken casting reels and from brass lures that were too worn to attract fish any longer. The handles of old table spoons can be made into hilts also, and the spoon part can be flattened to form a butt plate.

Nearly every cabinet shop has scraps of walnut, maple, and mahogany that are too small for their use, but perfect for yours. Even though these cabinet woods don't finish up as nicely as the exotic woods, their cost may be a deciding factor. Grips can also be made from bits and pieces of harness leather that you can often pick up for a song. Spacers can be fashioned from pieces of fiber such as used for electrical devices, and Plexiglas scraps are sometimes available from window and storm-door manufacturers.

For many years, my favorite handle material has been antlers from deer and elk that my friends or I have brought to bag. It has some disadvantages, true, but measured against these must be the satisfaction of having a knife handle with a history. In the chapter of handles, we talk about how antlers (i.e. stag) can be made into knife handles that are real beauties. Also, should your antlers be too small or crooked for an entire handle, their crowns make up into fine pommels. Consider them.

Another thing you want to think about is swapping. I have a hunting buddy who has ready access to small pieces of brass and aluminum. But because he travels a lot, he can't find the time to get into knife-making. The solution has been simple: He keeps me supplied with soft metal for hilts and pommels, and I make a good-looking knife for him every now and then.

There you have it. Getting started in knife-making involves little more than writing for some supply-house catalogs, ordering a blade or two and other accessories you may need, and taking inventory of what you have on hand. As you go along, you'll be surprised to find how many materials lend themselves to the knife-maker's art.

I do have one additional suggestion. If, like

me, you're a hunter and fisherman, plan your knife-making activities so that they fall between the close of hunting season and the opening of fishing season. That way, if you overlook the dog days of August, every year has just three fun seasons—hunting, fishing, and knife-making. I'm pretty sure that's the way the Good Lord intended for things to be arranged!

CHAPTER 6

BLADE DESIGN: Sizes, Shapes, and Grinds

The design, or configuration if you prefer, of knife blades has a history and romance all its own. Virtually every civilization has contributed its own distinctive design. The wickedly curved Kukris of the Nepalese mountain warriors known as Gurkhas, the serpentine krises of the Malaysian tribes, the richly ornamented daggers of the Middle East—all have contributed greatly to the lore that surrounds modern-day knife-making.

The nomenclature of knife blades follows as a logical consequence of design, being composed of descriptive terms needed to identify the configuration and grinds that are best suited to those jobs for which knives are made and used.

The popularity of different blade designs may not change as often as women's fashions. What does? But over the years, designs have come and gone—some of them more than once. Right now, the drop-point blade seems to be the style sought by many knowledgeable sportsmen. In the early

57

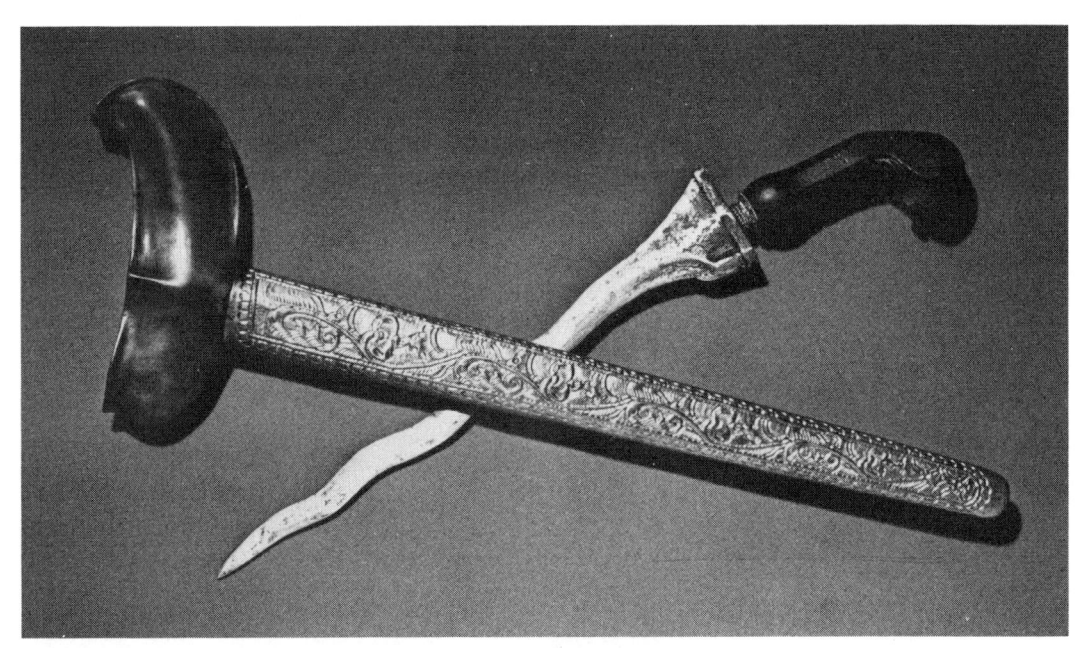

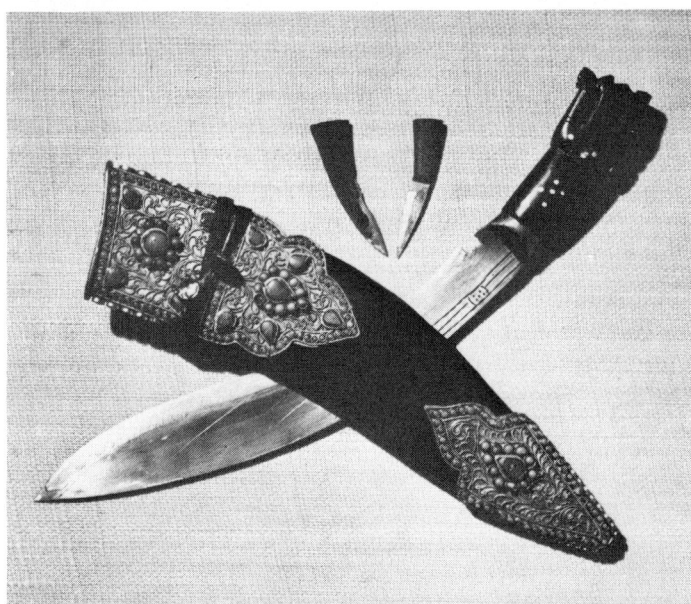

Although many countries and civilizations have contributed to contemporary knife design, some remain largely restricted to their country of origin. Shown here are the Malaysian kris (top), the Nepalese kukri (middle), and the Argentine gaucho knife (bottom). (Author's collection.)

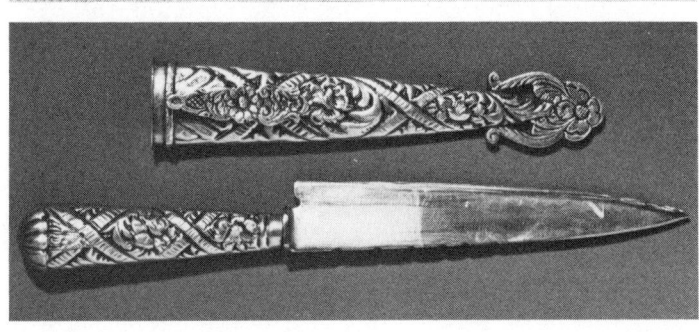

part of the 19th century, this was also true. But for a period of a hundred years or so in between, the clip-point blade, as epitomized by the Bowie knife, was what every hunter yearned for—or so it seemed from what the manufacturers were willing to provide.

There's a lot of human nature involved in what passes for popularity, whether the topic is women's fashions or blade design. Everyone wants what everyone else says is best, seldom pausing to consider whether it's really suited to the purpose. Only in recent years, and attributable almost entirely to the rebirth of custom knife-making, have manufacturers been prepared to offer more than one or two basic designs.

Nowadays, there are literally dozens of different combinations of sizes, shapes, and grinds to select from. And home hobbyists and custom grinders are expanding the number almost daily.

There's another factor to consider in the popularity of blade designs when viewed from the perspective of man's history and the advance of civilization. The demise of the fighting knife began about the time repeating firearms were invented, only to rise again when American soldiers found it necessary to learn the science of jungle warfare. The use of large, broad-blade skinners (à la Green River design) declined about the time we managed to decimate the western buffalo herds. And, as noted earlier, pure lack of interest in handmade quality occasioned by the industrialization of America brought a century-long malaise to quality cutlery.

Today's interest in knives, and manufacturers' response to that interest, springs—I suspect—from such ephemeral sources as nostalgia, greater leisure time, and a desire to own something that every other kid in the block doesn't have. It's the antithesis of industrialization.

THE EVOLUTION OF DESIGN

Looking again to history for a better understanding of how modern blade designs evolved, we might note that for several hundred years knives were carried almost exclusively as defensive weapons. It wasn't until the mid-1700s that English cutlers began producing knives that were intended for sporting purposes. (There was even a special blade for cutting the "brush" off the fox.)

Many of the early fighting knives were, in effect, little brothers of swords. The Roman dagger and the Scottish dirk were born of this legacy, as was the infamous "Arkansas toothpick" developed in the Confederacy about the time of the Civil War. The double-edged boot knife, favored by Mississippi River gamblers of the mid-to-late 19th century, was of similar origin.

The Scots, whose fighting history pre-dates medieval times, were perhaps the most direct in their approach: The Scotish claymore (or great sword), the dirk (or young sword) and the sgian dubh (or black-handled knife) comprised their trio of edged weapons.

The claymore was traditionally worn suspended over the right shoulder and on the left side, facilitating a cross-draw with the right hand while the left hand held the scabbard. The dirk was worn on the right side, either through the sash or sus-

This Arkansas toothpick with German silver hilt, aluminum spacers, brass butt cap, and curly maple handle is one of the author's favorite "wall hangers." A contemporary of the more famous Bowie knife, this design was a favorite of Confederate troops during the War Between the States. All components of the knife pictured here were supplied by Atlanta Cutlery Corp.

pended from a waist belt. The sgian dubh (Gaelic) was worn in the stocking, where it was the Highlander's weapon of last resort. (If you're wondering how to pronounce sgian dubh, the closest I can come phonetically is "skein due.") The Arkansas toothpick, which made its appearance in America

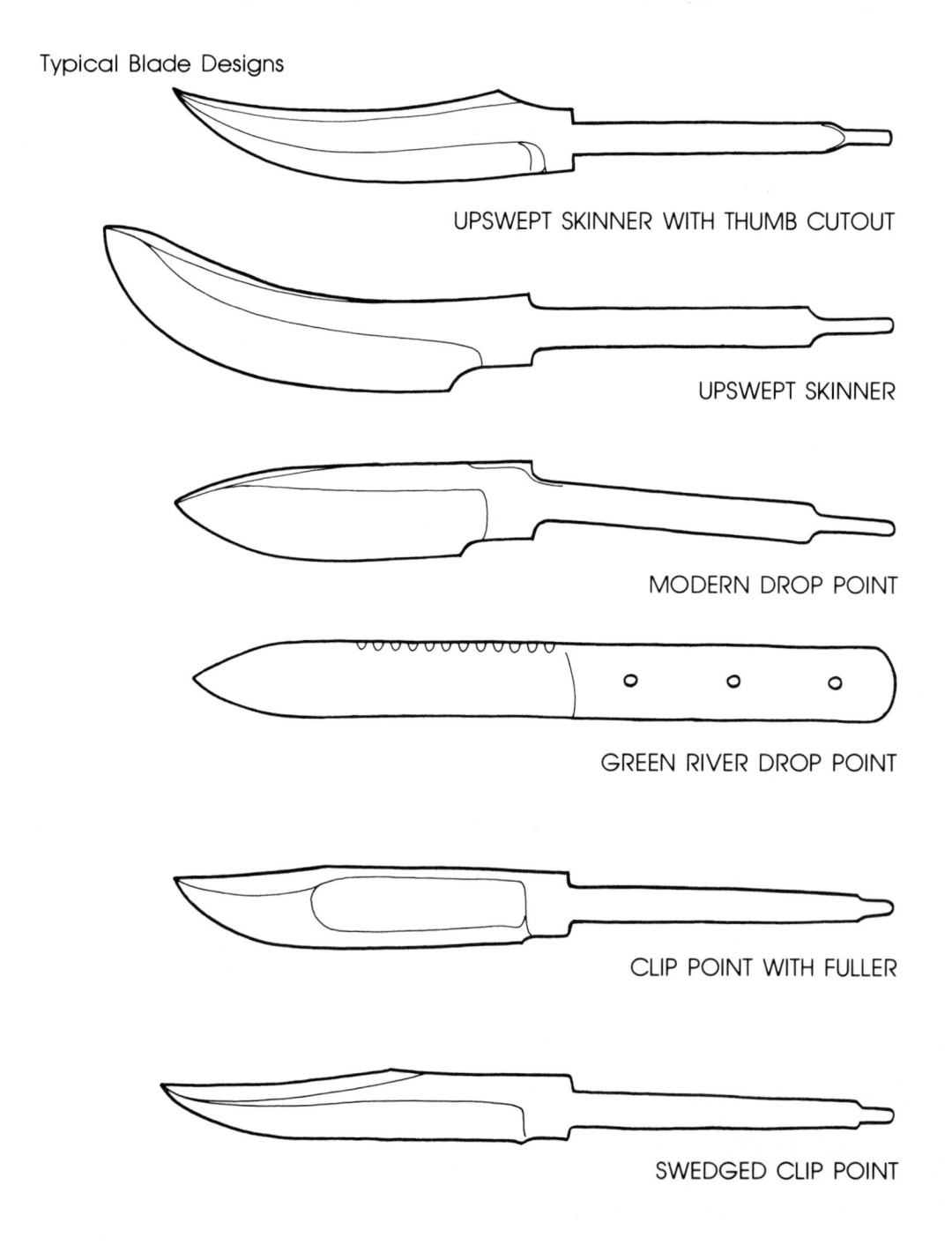

Typical Blade Designs

UPSWEPT SKINNER WITH THUMB CUTOUT

UPSWEPT SKINNER

MODERN DROP POINT

GREEN RIVER DROP POINT

CLIP POINT WITH FULLER

SWEDGED CLIP POINT

centuries later, appears to be a direct descendant of the sgian dubh, though I doubt the designers ever compared notes.

PURPOSE DETERMINES DESIGN

What is known today as the clip-point blade gained its greatest popularity in the Bowie knife which, as we have noted, influenced blade design for many years thereafter. Although sold as a hunting knife for several decades, the design is less adapted to skinning and other hunting chores than the drop-point, the upswept point, or the straight blade.

Most of the work in skinning is done with the forward two or three inches of the blade, and the clip-point, while fine for self-defense, always wants to head downhill. For light skinning chores, the drop-point is ideal, while the broad, fully upswept blade is great for bigger game. (Those buffalo skinners knew what they were doing with their Green River knives.)

The early-day fur-trappers and mountain men never knew when their knives would have to do double duty to dispatch a wayward Indian or ill-tempered grizzly. For this reason, they often favored blades that were 9 to 12 inches long. Today's deer hunter isn't likely to encounter such formidable opposition, and should select a blade of 3½ to 5 inches in length. As a matter of fact, if you want to get laughed right out of a Texas deerhunters' camp, try showing up with a 12-inch Bowie slung from your belt. I can guarantee the results.

SOME SPECIAL PURPOSE BLADES

There are a number of special purpose blades around, and we can nod to them in passing. I'll ignore that abomination known as the gut-hook, and the so-called Wyoming knife that looks more like a mixed-up fishhook than a blade. A useful special-purpose blade is the patch knife, used by black-powder aficionados to trim excess patching after the ball has been seated. Because they're intended to slice flush with the muzzle, these little blades are ground on one side only. This means that there's a left-hand and a right-hand to them, so if you make one, keep this in mind. I'm not into smoke-poles all that heavy, but I made a patch knife from one of Indian Ridge Trader's lightweight blanks that I use for cutting sheath leather. It works well for this purpose.

Throwing knives represent another specialized design. The critical factor in their design is that the weight of the knife must be well forward, which leads to a blade design that looks like a lopsided diamond or teardrop. Double-edged blades are the norm, but they need not be sharpened except two or three inches back from the point. No hilt is necessary, and handles are usually merely extended tangs or riveted scales.

SOME BASIC GRINDS

Along with the size and shape of your blade, there are half a dozen or so basic grinds that have quite a lot to do with how well your knife performs the chores for which you use it. Each grind has its own peculiar advantages and disadvantages as to honing ease, edge-holding ability, resistance to

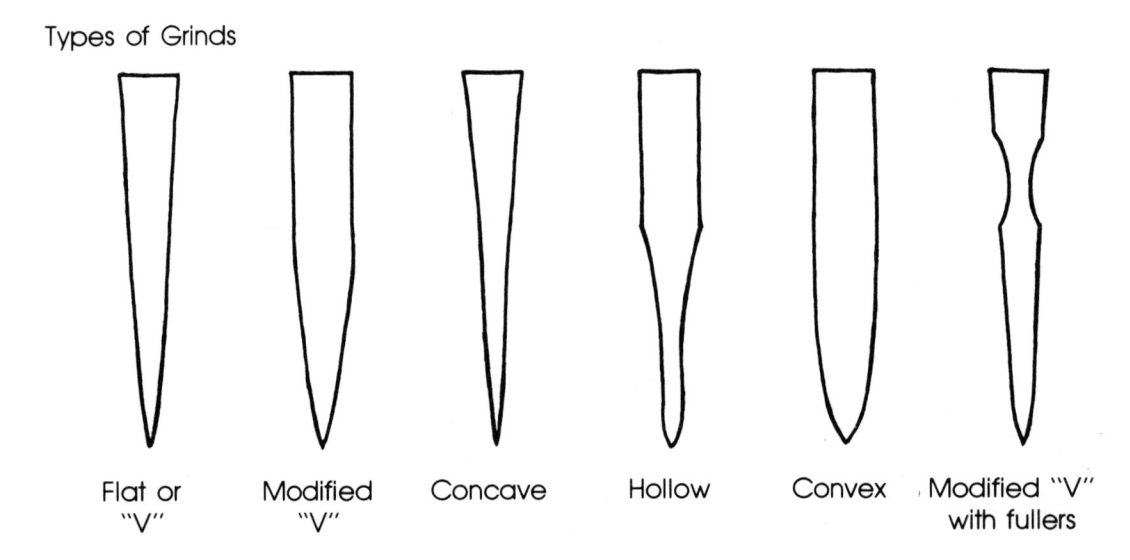

Types of Grinds

Flat or "V" Modified "V" Concave Hollow Convex Modified "V" with fullers abuse, and slicing ability. Just as there is no single knife-making steel that excels all others, there is no such thing as a "best" grind. Still, nearly everyone who has fooled around with knives for very long has developed some pretty strong ideas about which grind does which job best. Here are my views on the subject:

Flat or "V" grind — This is a good choice for skinning and carving; its slicing ability is above average. I'd rate its honing ease and edge-holding ability as good, but its resistance to abuse is only fair.

Modified "V" grind — I consider this to be the best grind for general-purpose use around the hunting camp. It's a little harder to hone than the flat grind, and its slicing ability isn't quite as good. Its edge-holding ability and resistance to abuse are excellent, however, which is why I rate it at the top of the heap as a general-purpose hunting blade.

Hollow grind — Over the years, I suspect there have been more honest differences of opinion about this grind than any other. I don't think anyone questions that its slicing ability is outstanding, and it's a joy to sharpen. I'd rate its edge-holding ability as fair to good. But the hollow-ground blade's resistance to abuse is not that great; hit a bone or use it as a pry, and you may have yourself a badly nicked blade. But if you are willing to give it tender care, the hollow-ground blade is unexcelled as a cutting tool.

Concave grind — This grind has a lot in common with the hollow grind; its slicing ease is excellent, but its resistance to abuse is poor. It is as easy to sharpen as the hollow-ground blade, but its edge life isn't much. Concave grinds once enjoyed considerable popularity as carving and skinning blades, but they've lost out to the hollow grind in recent years.

Convex grind — Because its edge life and resistance to abuse are outstanding, you'll find this grind used extensively for machetes, cane knives, and other blades designed for hacking. Sharpening is usually done with a file or coarse grindstone; you'll never shave with a convex grind. Slicing ease is obviously very poor.

Modified "V" with fullers — This is the grind used in the famous World War II "general-purpose" knife that Ka-Bar developed for the Marine Corps. You'll also run across some fullered blades with flat grinds, though I'm not sure why. Although fullers are sometimes called "blood grooves," their real purpose is simply one of weight reduction. The honing ease and slicing ability of a fullered blade is essentially the same as for the conventional modified "V" grind, but its resistance to abuse, assuming equal spine thickness, isn't quite as good.

CHAPTER 7

THE BLADE: Getting What You Want in a Handmade Knife

First off, let's all concede that grinding your own blades from old files and auto springs is a lousy way to make knives. Some of us did it back in the 30s and 40s because nothing else was available. But the knives we made then won't hold a candle to most of the blades that are available from today's knife-making supply houses.

Blades are available today in an unending variety of shapes, styles, and sizes, no less than a dozen types of steel, and at prices that are sure to fit everyone's pocketbook. Just thumbing through the catalogs and spec sheets of the suppliers is enough to quicken the pulse and gladden the heart of any dyed-in-the-wool knife fancier. Blades can be acquired from England, Sweden, Norway, Germany, Italy, Spain, Japan and, of course, the good old U.S. of A.

Back in frontier days, knives were fashioned at the blacksmith's forge as he hammered raw steel into the desired shape, ground it by hand, then annealed, hardened, and tempered it until the desired physical properties were obtained. With today's resurgence of interest in fine cutlery, a few master craftsmen have relearned—and improved on—this art that once was all but lost on this continent. These artists, some of whom have even reinvented the ancient art of making Damascus blades, are undoubtedly the crown princes of the knife-making world. Unfortunately, their prices are prohibitive for all but the wealthiest collectors, and waiting periods of two years are common.

FACTORY VERSUS HAND-GROUND BLADES

The other, far more common, method of custom knife-making involves taking a piece of hot-rolled or finish-ground mill stock and removing metal until the desired shape is at hand. In my opinion modern steel-making methods result in blades that are every bit as good as the best of the hand-forged products.

The main difference—and it's a big one—between today's factory blade and the handmade or custom blade is the amount of handiwork involved. Several good manufacturers boast of the handiwork that goes into their knives. Such statements, as far as they go, are correct. It's also accurate to say that a number of hand operations go into the assembly of an automobile. But I doubt that anyone would claim that Detroit's products are handmade.

When you buy a true handmade blade, it's largely the work of one man. When you buy a factory blade, it's usually the work of several men working in assembly line fashion and using jigs, dies, and other unromantic but laborsaving devices. About the only exception, to my knowledge, are the hand-ground blades that come out of the factories of Sheffield, England.

THE CHOICE IS YOURS

As a home hobbyist, it's your choice whether you want to work with a blade that has been entirely made by hand, one on which most of the work has been done by machines, or one which you grind yourself from blank stock. All are available, and all have their pros and cons.

I'm not sure that the handmade blade is all that much superior to the best of the factory blades. For sure, it's more romantic, and for sure it's more expensive. Prices for handmade blades start at better than $20 and go up pretty fast. It's possible to buy these blades as (1) blade alone (in which case you make your own hilt, handle, and pommel); (2) in kit form (in which case you do the final fitting and assembly); or (3) in finished form (in which case you supply nothing but money and can't claim to have made your own knife).

Handmade blades are available in several different designs and types of steel, including the Morseth line from A. G. Russell Company.

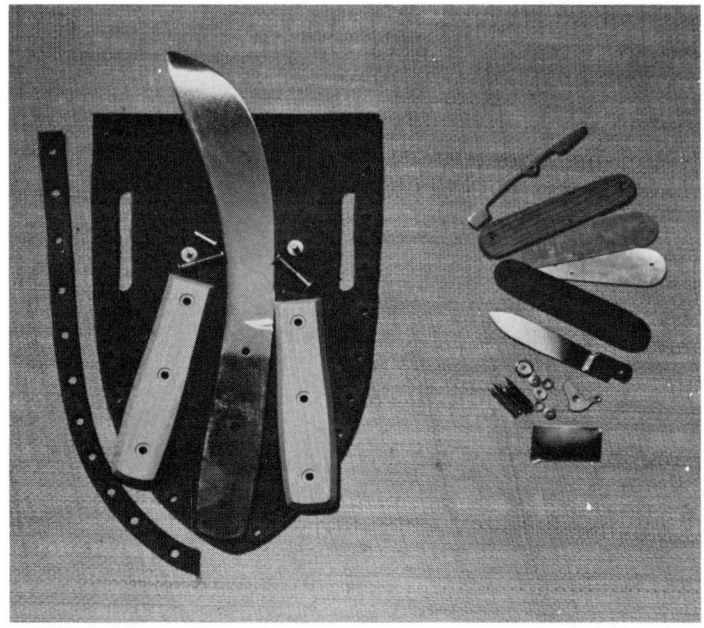

Knifemaking kits, such as these from Atlanta Cutlery Corp., simplify the art of knife-making, but limit the creativity of the home hobbyist. At left is a kit for assembling a buffalo skinner and sheath, and at right is a kit for assembling a single-blade folding knife. Kits are available in a wide variety of styles and prices, and provide a reasonable approach for the first-time knife-maker without a fully equipped workshop.

These truly superior blades are available in a broad variety of designs.

Factory-made blades range in quality and in price—the first usually being a function of the latter. The pick of the litter are probably the better Sheffield blades. And, as previously noted, I'm also enthusiastic about the Norwegian laminates from Atlanta Cutlery. Half a dozen full-tang styles from John Russell's original Green River Works are available from Indian Ridge Traders, and Bob Schrimsher's outfit (Custom Knifemaker's Supply) down in Texas offers a good selection of both U.S. and imported blades.

GRINDING YOUR OWN BLADE

Finally, there are the blades that you grind yourself from un-edged blanks or rolled stock. These are available as un-edged blades, where the tang has already been cut and drilled, or as rolled stock in several appropriate widths and thicknesses. Several types of steel, both tool and stainless, also are available. Schrimsher probably has the best selection in the latter category, and Indian Ridge Traders has a modest inventory of un-edged blade blanks.

Grinding your own blade undoubtedly results in a high quotient of self-expression, but it's not a simple undertaking. Before discovering the paste buffing compounds available from Cherry Corners, I would have sworn it couldn't be done without a bench-mounted belt sander. Now, by starting with a medium grade (36-grit) wheel on my bench grinder for shaping and initial grinding, then going to Cherry Corners' 240-grit or 320-grit compound and getting progressively finer, I find it can be done.

The previously extolled variable-speed hand drill, used with a 4-inch grinding wheel, also works well here, because its speed can be slowed down (about 900 RPM) to the point where you're

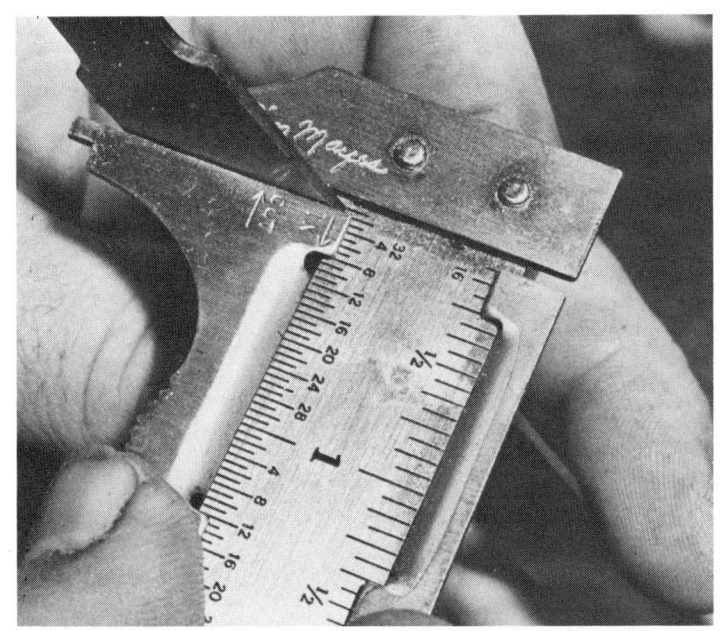

A. If you have the time and patience, there is a special satisfaction to be gained from grinding your own blade from a blank or from rolled stock. The Indian Ridge Traders' lightweight blank, which calipers a mere 1/16-inch thick, is a good project for the beginner. Here are the steps to follow:

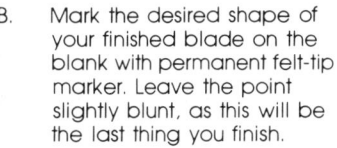

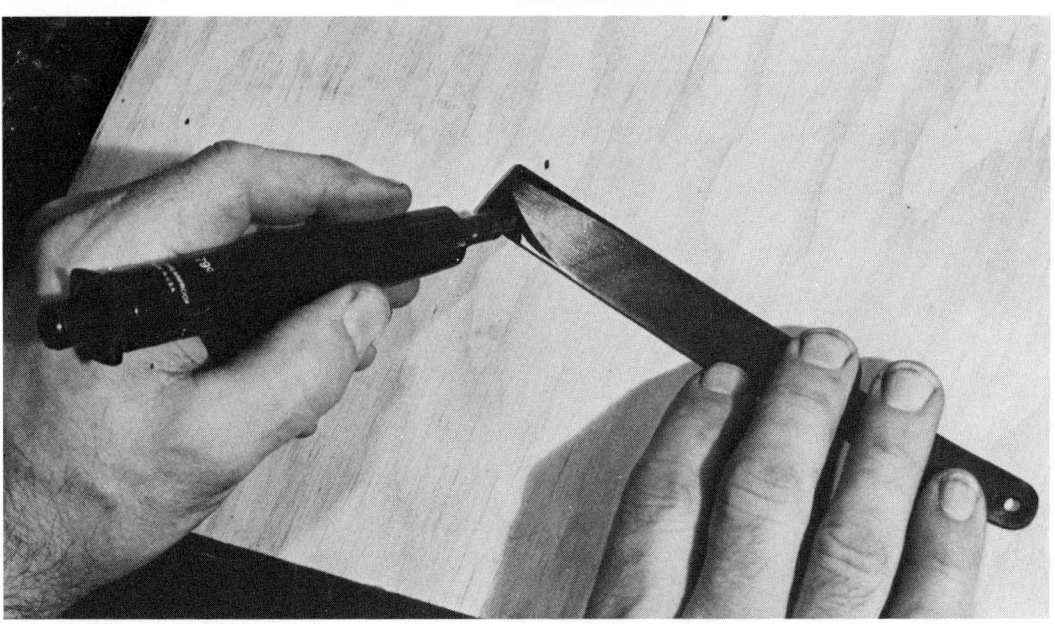

B. Mark the desired shape of your finished blade on the blank with permanent felt-tip marker. Leave the point slightly blunt, as this will be the last thing you finish.

not as apt to burn your work and ruin its temper. In my experience the medium-grit wheels don't seem to burn as rapidly as do the fine grades (60-grit and above). Just remember: Dip your blade in water every few seconds, and work barehanded. When the blade gets too hot to hold comfortably, you're approaching the danger point.

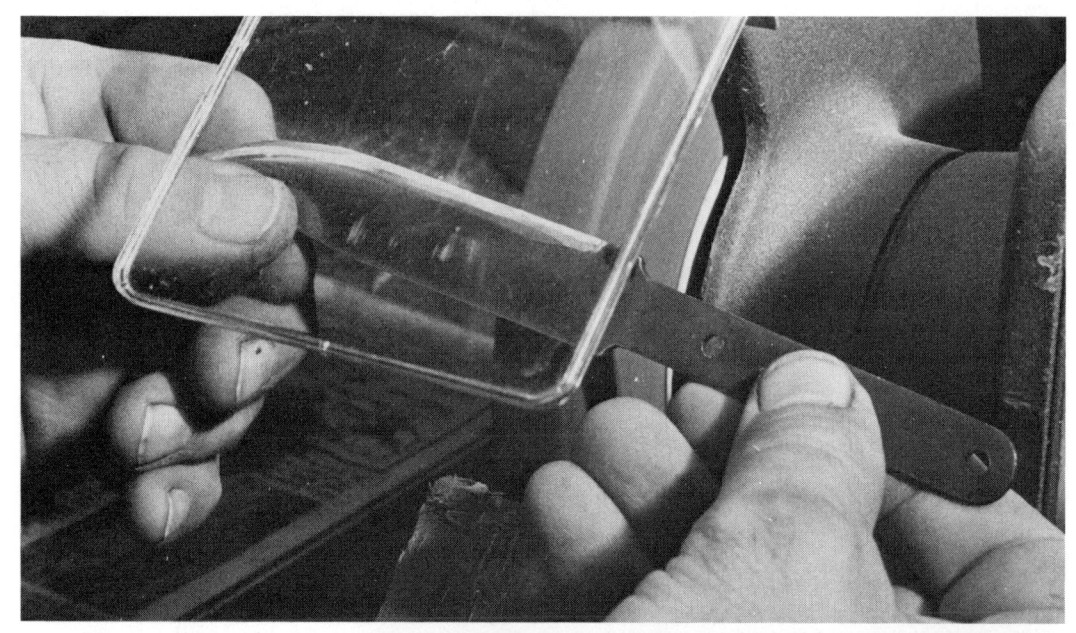

C. After shaping the blade to its approximate finished shape, begin grinding the edge, first one side and then the other. Begin with a medium grit wheel (approx. 36-grit); it is less likely to burn the blade than a finer grit.

D. Dip the blade in water every few seconds to prevent overheating that will ruin the temper. Unlike rolled stock, blanks are hardened and tempered when you receive them; this lowers the cost but requires additional care.

With blade grinding, as with so many other endeavors, practice makes perfect. Don't get discouraged if you mess up a piece of steel and have to start over. Even the pros toss out lots of ruined blades. Knife steel isn't very expensive, running currently about $5 or $6 per linear foot in popular widths and thicknesses. You won't need a metal-

E. As grinding progresses, bevel is moved further and further back from the edge and toward the spine. If flat-ground blade is desired, taper should extend uniformly from edge to spine; if modified "V" grind is used, bevel should extend about one-half width of blade, or at least one-half inch from cutting edge if working with wider blade. Swedge or false-edge may also be added if desired.

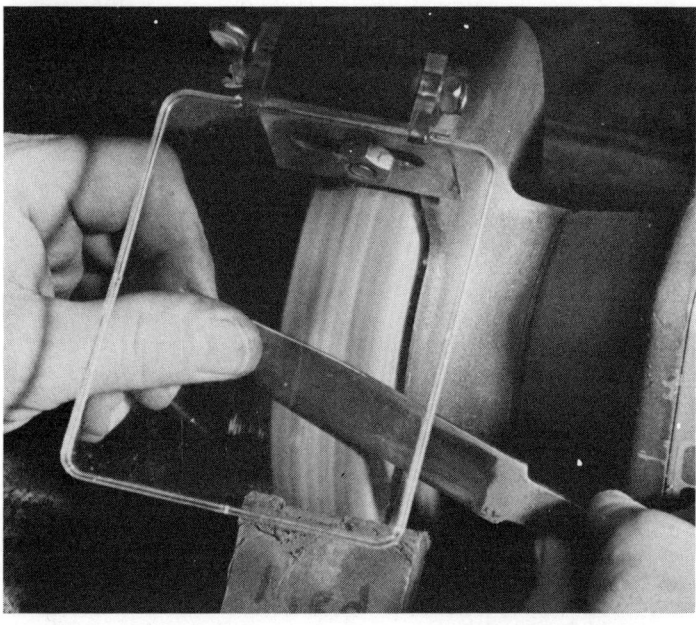

F. With bevel nearly completed, move from grinding wheel to buffing wheel dressed with 320-grit or 240-grit compound. When bevel has reached desired configuration, move to buffing wheel dressed with 600-grit compound and remove grind marks.

cutting bandsaw if you start with stock that approximates the width of your finished blade.

When ordering stock or un-edged blanks, keep in mind that the thinner it is, the easier it is to work with. I recommend Indian Ridge Traders' lightweight blank for your initial effort; it calipers a mere 1/16-inch thick.

Modified "V" grinds are the most practical for the home hobbyist, but you can produce a flat-ground blade if you really want to work at it. We're talking about a full day's effort, though, so don't get into it unless you have time and patience. Unless you're careful, what you'll wind up with is a convex grind and mediocre slicing ability. Hollow grinds require specialized equipment, and a skill that is beyond the scope of this book.

You can put any sort of tang you want on your hand-ground blade, but full and short tangs are easiest because they require less metal removal. The rolled stock you buy hasn't been hardened (you'll have to send it off for heat treatment), so you won't have too much difficulty drilling the tang. IRT's lightweight blank comes with a short

G. Flat-ground blade is ready for buffing with brown and red rouge. Author also finds it useful to hand-grind blade on a bench stone at this point. If mirror rather then satin finish is desired, final step will be polishing with felt wheel dressed with white rouge.

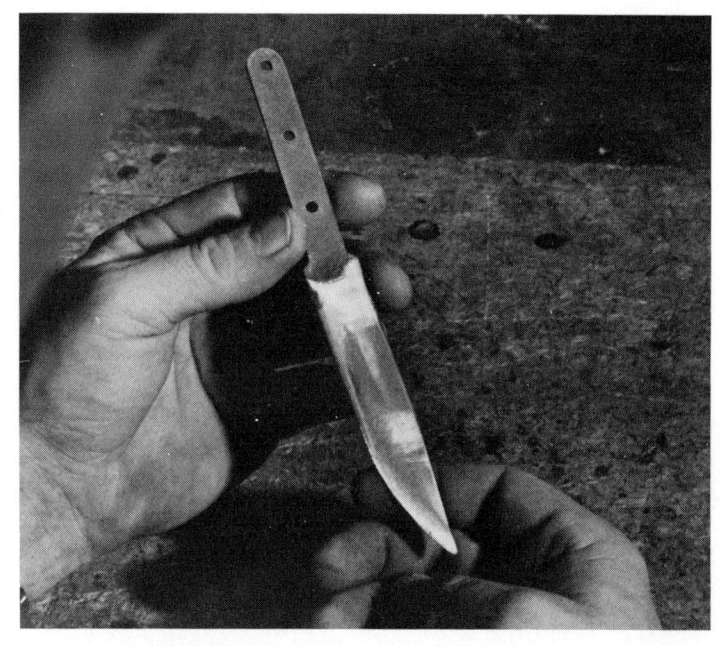

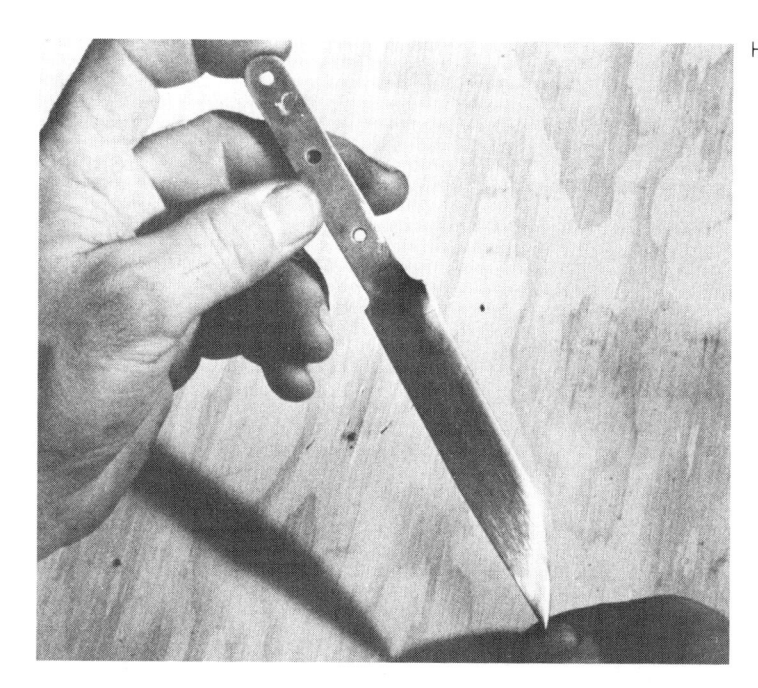

H. Finished blade will now have hilt soldered in place and handle affixed.

tang that is predrilled with three rivet holes. The tang is hardened along with the blade, so you'll wear out a couple of bits trying to drill it.

As previously noted, I use a 36-grit grinding wheel and Cherry Corners' compound to get my blades started. These are all you'll need for a modified "V" grind, but if you want to flat grind your blade, you'll likely spend some time on a coarse-grit carborundum bench stone as well. I alternate between a bench stone and the medium-grit buffing wheel, then finish with red rouge buffing compound and a soft Arkansas oilstone. There's more on blade finishing in Chapter 14.

Two areas of the blade require special attention. The ricasso is tough to handle on a grinding wheel, so I get mine started with a mill file and dress it from time to time with a flat needle file. The point is also difficult, because it burns the easiest. You can overcome this difficulty to some extent by waiting until the final finishing to put a fine point on the blade. Keep this in mind as you do your initial shaping.

THE VIRTUES OF LAMINATED STEEL

Just about every knife-maker it seems, has his own favorite steel. For some experts, the highly alloyed stainless products have no peer. Others swear by high-carbon tool steel. I have no quarrel with their choices, but for me the laminated steels from Norway offer everything a knife blade should have.

I like the Norwegian laminates for several reasons: The blade will sharpen easily, yet hold a good edge; it will withstand all sorts of abuse; and it buffs to one of the nicest satin finishes that lasts through long use and repeated sharpenings.

Another big (to me) advantage of laminated steel is its price. Atlanta Cutlery offers a modest selection of laminated factory blades for prices that range from about $3 to $10. If you want to go a little higher up the price scale, A. G. Russell offers a good choice of handground laminated blades that range from about $22 to $33. This is Russell's famous Morseth line, available also in kit form or as finished knives at substantially higher prices. One problem with the Morseth line is that you sometimes have to wait six months or so to get the design you want.

The secret behind the laminated blade lies in its construction. The core is a hard steel that tests in the high 50s on the Rockwell "C" scale, and the outer layers are softer steel that tests several points lower. Don't tell me those Norwegians aren't a clever folk.

CHAPTER 8

HEAT TREATMENT: Giving Your Blade Its Character

Second only to the composition of the steel it contains, heat treating has more to do with the physical properties of your knife blade than anything else. All forms of heat treating are pretty highly specialized, and there's precious little of it that can (or should) be undertaken by the home hobbyist. Still, a fundamental understanding of how heat affects steel is basic to any discussion of knife-making.

We all know that heat is used in the initial conversion of iron ore to pig iron, and from pig iron to steel. These are manufacturing processes though, and not what we're talking about here at all. The heat-treating processes we're interested in are those that are applied to finished steel at or about the time it is being forged or ground into its final shape.

Specifically, the processes we're interested in are *hardening, annealing,* and *tempering.* Of the three, only tempering can be undertaken by the hobbyist, and that only on an experimental or "have-to" basis. Nevertheless, if you'll forgive me, I'm going to mention in passing how we used to try to anneal and harden blades made from files and such back in the dark ages of the thirties and forties.

Let me mention also, that rather than get involved in a bunch of definitions that tend to slow us both down, I've included most of them in the glossary. So if you get sort of bogged down, flip back and take a more precise look at what I'm talking about.

By far the most common method of heat-treating today involves the use of specially controlled furnaces (with thermocouples and indicating pyrometers) designed for nothing else. Lest you be tempted to rush out and buy one for your very own, the cheapest of them starts at about $350, and that's not even a very good one.

There are half a dozen different types of heat-treating furnaces on the market, but except for the source of heat (i.e., gas, electric, etc.) and temperature ranges, all of them do about the same thing. That is, they heat metal to temperatures as high as 2,500 degrees F and keep it there under carefully controlled conditions.

HEAT-TREATING SERVICES

There are a number of firms and some knife-makers which specialize in heat-treating. Methodology differs broadly from one type of steel to the next, so even if you should progress to the point where you require the services of a heat-treating firm, it's best to deal with one that specializes in knife blades. A couple of them are listed in the appendix.

Not even all professional knife-makers elect to do their own heat-treating, which should tell us something about how specialized an area it is. In their case, however, it's largely a matter of economics; you've got to heat-treat an awful lot of blades before it'll pay you to shell out a thousand bucks or so for a good furnace. The firms that do specialize in heat-treating, though, usually charge only $4 or $5 a blade.

You won't need the services of a heat-treating firm unless you get into grinding your own blades from rolled stock or forged (unfinished) blades. Blade blanks available from a few suppliers are already heat treated, with hard blades and drilled tangs. If you ever do send a blade to be treated, the folks you send it to have got to know what kind of steel it's made from. If you don't know that, forget it.

HOW BLADES ARE HARDENED

Knife blades (and other steel of course) are hardened by bringing them to a red-hot heat and then *quenching* them in water, oil, air, or brine.

The whole idea behind quenching is to cool the metal rapidly and keep it from passing through its *recalescence* stage or point. This is the basic difference between annealing and hardening—the speed at which the metal is cooled.

Quenching forces metal to retain the desired molecular structure or grain size. That's why the quenching medium is so important. In the chapter on metallurgy we mentioned water-hardening steels, etc. If, for example, a water-hardening steel were to be quenched in oil, it would cool too slowly and wouldn't attain its maximum hardness. If on the other hand, an oil-hardening steel were cooled too quickly as in water, it would likely crack or warp. It all makes sense, when you stop to think about it.

PHYSICAL PROPERTIES OF STEEL

I'm going to get a tiny bit technical now, so you can pass over this part if you want to. I just don't want someone popping up a hundred years from now and saying old Uncle Jim didn't give 'em all the facts.

Steel that hasn't yet been heat-treated is called *pearlite*. (Remember, check out the glossary!) During the hardening process, its molecular structure is tranformed to a type of steel known as *austenite.* This is a mode that exists (temporarily, of course) between the steel's lower and upper *critical temperature points.* The desired molecular structure of fully hardened steel is obtained when the austenite is quenched, at which time it takes on the properties of steel called *martensite.* The latter is characterized by the needlelike pattern of its molecules. At this point, the steel is extremely hard, but it's also extremely brittle. As we'll see in a moment, tempering is what gets rid of the brittleness.

REPRESENTATIVE QUENCHING TEMPERATURES

High-carbon steels (the kind that knives are made from) reach their *decalescence* point—that is, transform from pearlite to austenite—at 1,330 degrees F. More complex (highly alloyed) steels generally reach their decalescence points at somewhat higher temperatures. For example:

Water-hardening steels are quenched at about 1,450 to 1,500 degrees F.

Oil-hardening steels are quenched at temperatures of 1,500 to 1,550 degrees F.

Air-hardening steels are quenched at temperatures of 1,600 to 1,775 degrees F.

And the very highly alloyed steels, such as stainless, may be brought to temperatures as high as 2,500 degress F before quenching—usually in oil but sometimes in air.

THE REASON FOR ANNEALING

Temperatures used to anneal steel are very close to those used to harden it. The difference, as I've indicated, is that the cooling process is done rapidly for hardening, and very slowly for annealing.

Annealing softens steel, but it also relieves some of the internal stresses and strains caused by previous operations. Steels that have been forged must be annealed before they can be hardened. This process is known as *normalizing.*

Annealing involves heating the steel to just

above its upper critical temperature point (*full annealing*) or just below its lower critical temperature point *(process annealling)*. In either case the metal is cooled slowly, so that it passes through its recalescence point, by placing it in sand or lime.

WHY BLADES ARE TEMPERED

Steel that has been hardened must then be *tempered* or *drawn* to remove its brittleness and increase its toughness. This is usually done after all but the final grinding and machining has been done.

The degree of toughness (i.e. lack of brittleness) that is obtained by tempering depends entirely on the temperature to which the blade is heated. It has nothing to do with how quickly or slowly it is cooled.

Tempering, unlike hardening and annealing, is a relatively simple process that can be done by the home hobbyist working with a propane torch. Three factors work for you here:

First, the temperatures are much lower; sec-

Most, but not all, blades are received from the supplier with hardened blades and annealed tangs. Note that the round tang of this small dagger made in Sheffield, England, has been threaded and a single pin-hole drilled. A small double-hilt, made from a silver tablespoon, also has been soldered to the tang. The dagger will be completed with the wood block and brass butt cap, also pictured.

ond, the ranges aren't as critical; and third, the colors that steel passes through as it is heated give a very close approximation of the temperature to which it has been heated.

The following chart relates color changes to temperature ranges. The range from 510 to 530 degrees F (purple color) is about right for most knife blades. With the thought that you may occasionally want to temper some of your workbench tools, I've included ranges and colors for other items as well. (A cautionary word: This chart is not correct for stainless steels; so don't try it on them.)

TEMPER COLORS FOR CARBON STEELS

Color	Fahrenheit Temperatures	Use
Pale yellow	400°	Lathe and shaping tools
Light straw	430°–450°	Drill bits and reamers
Tan (dark straw)	450°–470°	Taps and dies
Brown	470°–500°	Shears and scissors
Brownish purple	500°–510°	Axes and wood chisels
Purple	510°–530°	Knives and cold chisels
Bright blue	530°–560°	Screwdrivers
Dark blue	560°–600°	Wood saws
Black	600° plus	Too hot; retreating required

As you can see from the chart, the higher the tempering temperature, the more brittleness and hardness are reduced. Hardness and toughness are trade-offs, one against the other. And while you don't need a knife blade that is as hard as a high-speed drill bit, neither do you want one so soft it won't hold an edge. The composition of your steel, the hardening process to which it is subjected and finally, how it is tempered, and what makes the difference in the way your knife does its job.

HOMESTYLE HEAT-TREATING

Now for that historical note on how we used to heat-treat our blades back in the "good ol' days."

Soft metals, such as brass, are not tempered, and may therefore be ground or heated without fear of destroying their temper. This cast-brass hilt is being ground to shape while held in vise-grip pliers. This practice should never be followed, however, when drawn steel is being worked. With tempered blades, bare hands are the rule.

Mr. Jackson, the blacksmith friend and mentor of my youth, explained to me patiently one day that a rule-of-thumb method for heat-treating small steel parts was to put 'em on a horseshoe magnet and heat them with an oxyacetylene torch until they fell off. He didn't know the technical explanation for this, but he figured it would be easier for me than judging the proper quenching point by the cherry-red color, as he did.

I didn't discover until years later that steel loses its magnetism when it reaches its decalescence point, which is the reason it falls off the magnet.

But anyhow, I tried it one Saturday with an old magnet I got from a buddy whose dad worked for the phone company, and a bucket of used motor oil. I didn't have anything remotely resembling a Rockwell tester, or anything else for that matter. But the blade did seem to hold an edge and sharpen a mite better after my home-grown treatment.

I was pleased as punch until I told the old man. He snorted and allowed as how I was lucky not to have blown the whole place sky-high. And that was the end of my budding career as a professional knife-maker. Maybe that's what Mr. Jackson had in the back of his mind all along.

CHAPTER 9

THE TANG:
Its Purpose
and Design

The tang of a knife serves a single function: to affix the handle to the blade. Yet, strangely enough, you will find more contradictory opinion expressed on what constitutes the best tang design than almost any other part of the knife.

Some knife-makers swear that only the full tang imparts sufficient strength, and will make no other kind. Others are equally adamant about the threaded round tang or its modifications. Yet in the final analysis, the type of tang, like the blade, depends upon your own personal choice and the method of construction you have in mind.

There are four basic tangs, but each can be modified extensively to suit your individual tastes and requirements. Let's look at them one at a time:

The full tang — In its simplest form, the full tang is unquestionably the easiest to work with. With it, all that's required to complete a crude but serviceable knife are two scales riveted or pinned to its sides. This was the way the famous Green River knives were made, and they served yeoman duty throughout the West for half a century. This is also how most kitchen cutlery is made.

Pinholes for Scales →

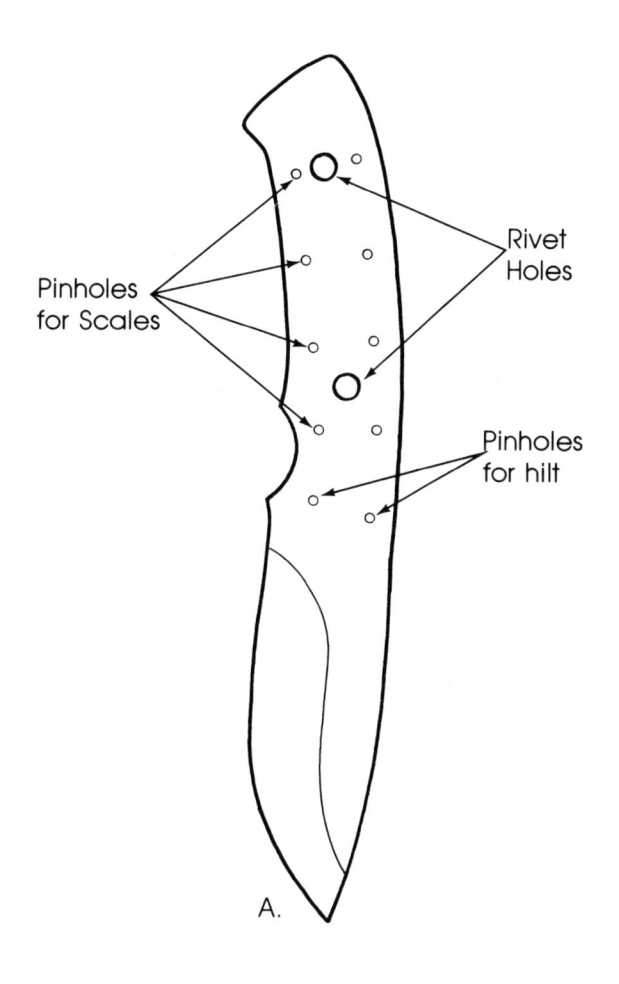

Rivet Holes →

Pinholes for hilt →

A.

Types of Tangs
Full Tang
Round Tangs
Short Tang
Modified Tang

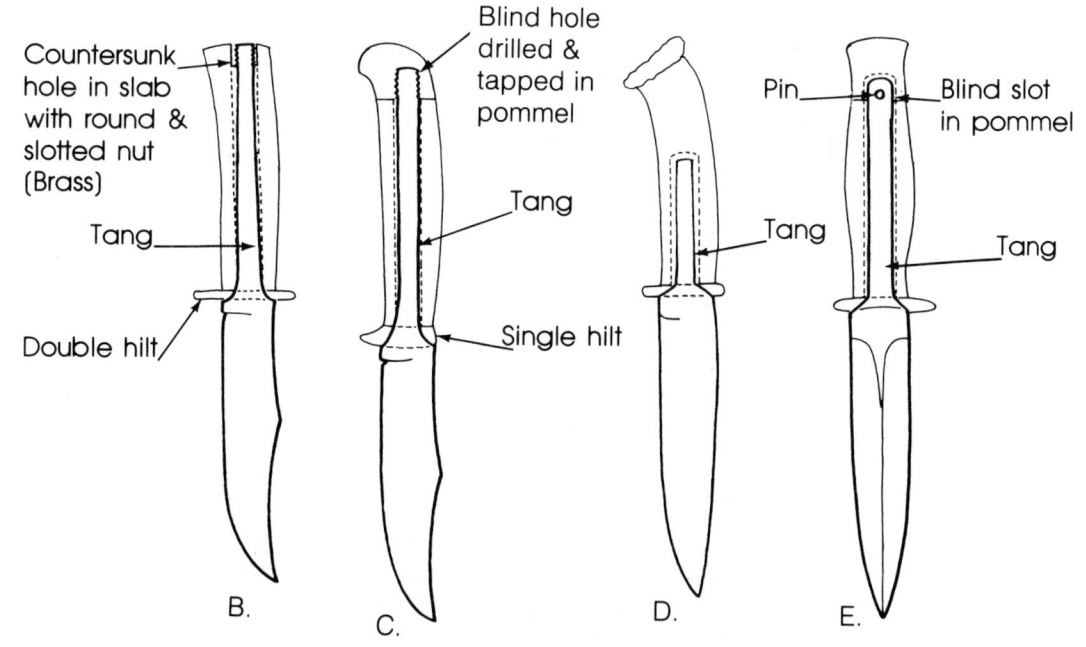

Countersunk hole in slab with round & slotted nut (Brass)

Tang

Double hilt

B.

Blind hole drilled & tapped in pommel

Tang

Single hilt

C.

Tang

D.

Pin — **Blind slot in pommel**

Tang

E.

83

The full-tang design is also well adapted to the use of a double hilt or guard, as with the classic Bowie knife design. If a single-hilt design is desired, a fully slotted or split-end hilt design must be used, as the width of the tang is approximately the same as the width of the blade where it meets the tang. Several variations of this design are possible. Accompanying illustrations that begin on page 90 demonstrate better than words what this design looks like. Split-end hilts may be soldered or pinned in place.

The round tang — The "round" tang is not actually round, but rectangular in shape for most of its length. Only the upper inch or so of the tang is actually round, and this portion is usually threaded to accept a tapped pommel. Some round tangs are threaded at the factory, but on most you will find it necessary to file the end of the tang to perfectly round dimensions, then thread it yourself with a die of appropriate size.

Most, but not all, factory-threaded tangs are made to receive a standard 10×24 machine-screw thread, so readily available drills and taps can be used for preparing the pommel material. Taps and dies can be purchased individually (be sure you get matching sizes) or in sets that contain a dozen or so in assorted sizes. Because tangs are made of soft (unhardened) steel and the pommel material of soft metal, the inexpensive imported tap-and-die sets are adequate for most knife-making purposes.

Use of a round tang usually presupposes the use of a stick or block for the handle. When this construction method is used, one or two parallel holes are drilled the entire length of the stick, and the tang is inserted through them. This should be done *before* any shaping work is done on the handle. Long, straight sections of stag are suited to this construction method, and round-tang construction is requisite to handles made of leather.

I prefer another type of handle construction, even when using a round tang. The way I do it is to either split the slab and inlet just enough space to receive the tang, or to start with scales like in full-tang construction. These too must be inlet. I then epoxy and pin the split slab or scales to fully enclose the tang. A tapped pommel or butt plate is then added to complete the knife.

The round tang is still the favored method of construction for "store-bought" hunting knives, though its use is not as total as it once was.

The modified round tang — This is the tang used in the famous Buck knives, which alone speaks well of its acceptance. The modified tang suggests the use of a pommel with a blind slot that is pinned to a hole in the upper portion of the tang. This is the system used by Buck. Another excellent approach is to inlet equally two scales, which then completely enclose the tang. For added strength, I prefer to both epoxy and rivet or pin the scales, with at least some of the pins or rivets passing through the tang.

The effect is the same as with the inlet round tang, except no threaded portion is present to receive a tapped pommel. A slotted pommel may again be used, or the handle material can be extended to enclose the entire tang. If the latter method is used, the handle is contoured to form its own "pommel," or the handle is finished straight.

The short tang — This type of tang is merely a round or modified tang that has been shortened to approximately three-quarters of its original length. Some knife-makers maintain that this method of construction is inherently weak, but its use by several prominent designers (including the excellent Smith & Wesson line) leads me to accept it as basically sound. Its acceptability lies in the availability of the excellent epoxys that are on today's market.

The use of a short tang offers several interesting possibilities. One, of course, is the storage space in the handle, characterized by several of the Smith & Wesson offerings. Another feature is the short tang's adaptability to curved handles, frequently fashioned from deer antlers. Slab or scale construction is possible using the short tang, and pins or rivets can, of course, be used in addition to epoxy.

When stick handles are used with the short tang, it is good to grind or file alternating angled slots (I call them "teeth") in the tang for better holding power. The drilled handle is epoxied to the tang, which we'll discuss further in Chapter 11.

MODIFYING YOUR TANG

Just because the supplier's catalog doesn't list the tang configuration with the blade you have in mind, don't be deterred from specifying that particular blade. Any larger tang can be converted—by sawing, grinding, or filing—to any smaller tang. It's also possible by using sheet brass of aluminum, to convert a short tang to a full tang. The softer metal is simply soldered or epoxied to the tang to give the shape you want. For an alternative, especially should you want to add a touch of color to your handle, separate the scales with spacer material of fiber or Plexiglas. Both are available in several colors and thicknesses. Once the scales are epoxied and pinned or riveted, this arrangement is almost as strong as a full-tang composed entirely of steel.

The tangs of better blades are usually annealed so you can saw, drill, file, and thread them without undue wear to your tools. Before basing your design on the supposition that the tang is annealed, however, check by drilling a test hole.

It's also possible to bend round tangs to obtain desired handle angles—something that seems to be increasingly popular in knife design.

To bend the tang, place the knife in a vise, heat the tang with a torch, and peen it rapidly but lightly with a medium-weight (16-oz) ball peen hammer. Alternatively, the tang can usually be bent by inserting it in a pipe of appropriate size and applying steady pressure while heating the tang. A word of caution here: When you heat your tang, you *must* use heat-control paste on the blade to avoid ruining its temper.

When drilling the tang to receive pins or rivets, you naturally want to use high-speed bits even though the metal is relatively soft. Also lubricate the drill hole with cutting or light machine oil as you drill.

CHAPTER 10

HILTS AND POMMELS: How to Make Them

In Chapter 2 we discussed the hilt, or guard, of a knife, which is the crosspiece that safeguards your hand from slipping on to the blade, and the pommel or butt cap, which is the part that crowns the handle. Not all knives have or need hilts or pommels, but they are attractive and utilitarian features of most hunting and fighting knives.

Three soft metals—brass, aluminum, and nickel silver—are commonly used for making hilts and pommels. The same metal is usually used for both parts on any given knife but there's nothing sacrosanct about this arrangement. I've often used brass for the guard and aluminum for the pommel, simply because it gives better weight distribution to the knife. Strict traditionalists may frown on such mixed marriages, but they can do their thing and I'll do mine.

Extremely attractive pommels can also be made from stag crowns, particularly when used in combination with wood or leather handles of contrasting color. This use of stag crowns also solves the problem of what to do with antlers from spike bucks, or misshaped antlers too crooked for handle material. Buck knives use an aluminum-base alloy known as duraluminum for its hilts and pommels, and this is undeniably great stuff. However, its age-hardening characteristics dictate that it must be kept at subzero temperatures prior to use, which renders its use by home hobbyists impractical.

Each of the three commonly used hilt-and-pommel metals have their own advantages and disadvantages. Brass is sufficiently hard to resist indentation in normal service, but it is heavy and tends to imbalance your knife when used excessively. (Browning, for example, sells an excellent knife, but their use of a large brass pommel makes their knives extremely butt-heavy, a feature I find undesirable.)

Aluminum overcomes the weight disadvantage of brass but it is easily scratched and dented. Nickel silver offers a nice compromise between brass and aluminum, but it is more expensive than either of them and somewhat more difficult to work. As usual you pay your money and you take your choice.

Pommels can be made from a variety of materials — from soft metals such as brass, aluminum or nickel (German) silver to crowns cut from deer or elk antlers. The commonly used metals are further available, as shown here, as castings or rolled or bar stock.

MAKING THE HILT

There are essentially two approaches to hilt making—you can work from, first, bar stock of appropriate width and thickness or, second, you can purchase rough castings that still require considerable grinding, filing, and buffing to complete. A third approach, essentially a modification of the first, is to work with materials that you have on hand. As noted earlier, old casting-reel cranks, discarded tableware, brass fishing lures, and sundry other odds and ends are all candidates for conversion.

Working with bar or sheet metal gives the hobbyist his greatest latitude for innovation, because the configuration of the hilt is limited only by his own imagination. At the same time, knife-maker supply houses are pretty innovative folks themselves, and there are mighty few shapes and sizes of guards not available in cast form. The accompanying photo illustrates some of them. These things are as rough as a corncob when you get them, but with grinding, sanding, and buffing they finish up slick as a whistle.

A good selection of cast hilts, in either brass or nickel silver, is available from the knife-making supply houses. Shown here are single, double, tapered-quillon, and split-end hilts.

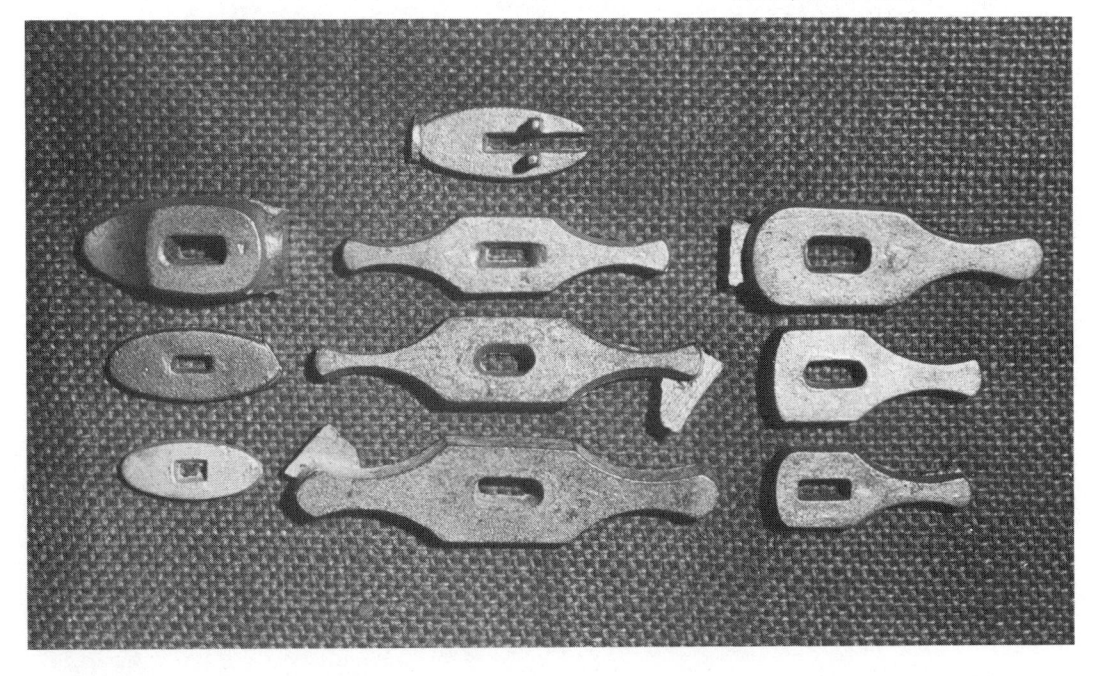

Two thicknesses of stock commonly used for hilts are ¼-inch and ⅜-inch. The former is used in its original thickness, and the latter is ground or filed to produce tapered quillon(s). Stock as thin as ⅛-inch and as thick as ⅝-inch is also carried by the supply houses, and castings can be had in several sizes and thicknesses.

The whole idea, of course, is to fit the size and

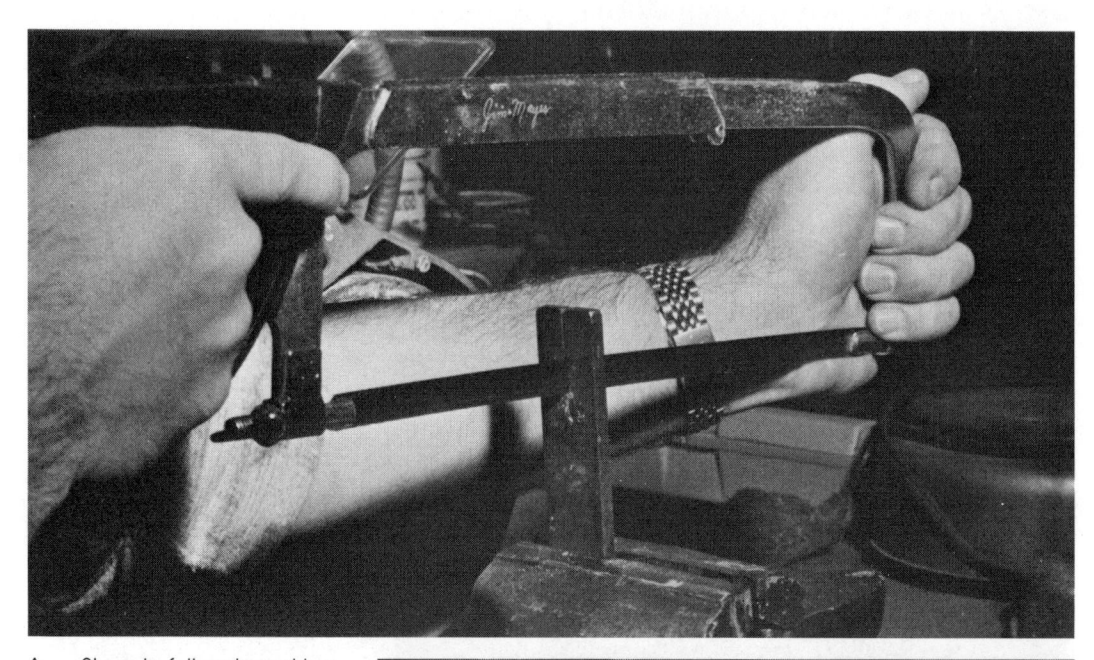

A. Steps to follow in making split-end hilt from bar stock: Scribe center line and make cut with hacksaw.

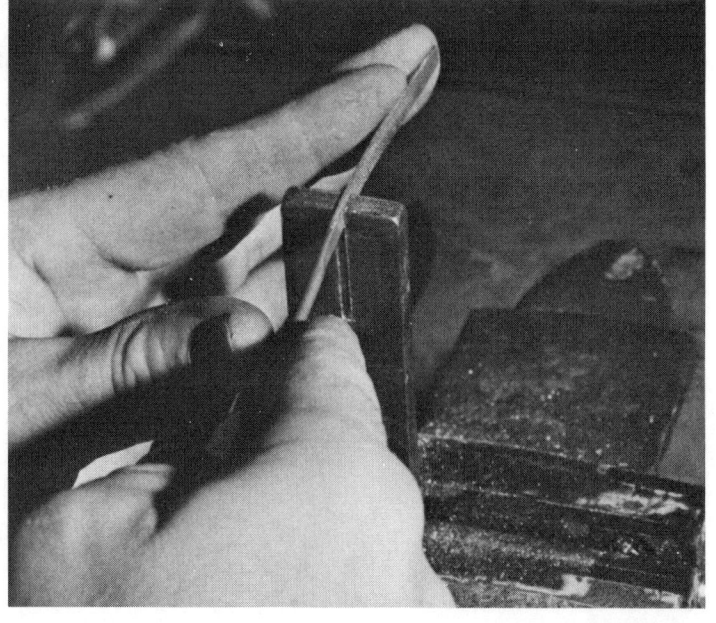

B. Enlarge saw cut with needle file.

shape of the hilt to the size and design of the knife. Within reason, if it's pleasing to the eye, it's right for the purpose.

Your first step in making a hilt from bar stock is to scribe a line down the middle of the metal you intend to use. The scribed line should be as long as your tang is wide. Next, use a center punch to indent both ends of the line, and at intermediate points along the line. The indentations should be about as far apart as the tang is wide.

Now select a drill bit that is slightly smaller than the thickness of the tang, and drill out the hilt along the line you have marked and punched. Be sure the stock is held securely in a machinist's vise, and begin with the end holes. You will, upon completion, have drilled out a slot that is nearly as long as the tang is wide, and parallel to the sides of the stock. If some metal remains between the drilled holes (it usually does), remove this with a cold chisel or tungsten carbide cutter mounted in your Moto-Tool.

Use a flat needle file to enlarge the slot to the precise dimensions of the tang. Go slow and use care; the effectiveness of the soldering job that is to follow depends on how good a job you do now.

Complete enlarging slot with small mill file.

D. Saw hilt to appropriate length.

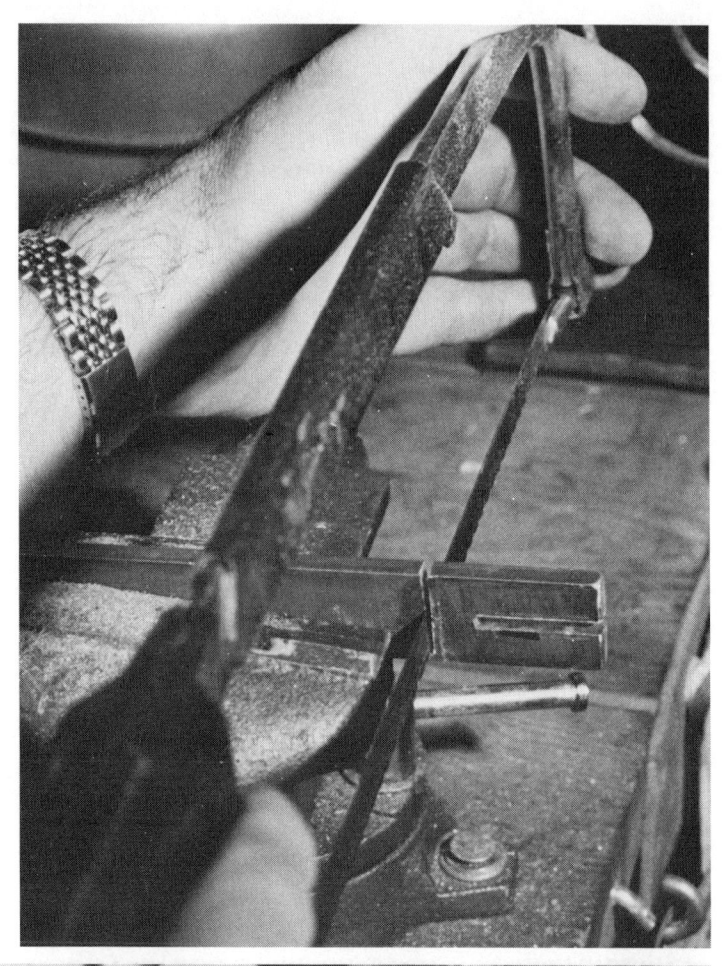

E. Rough grind hilt on bench-mounted grinder.

Test the fit several times as you proceed, and get it just as close as possible.

There is one exception to the procedure just described, and that is if you are working with a full-tang. This method of construction requires the use of an open or split-end hilt that slides horizontally on to the tang, rather than down its length. If a split-end hilt is what you need, the slot can be cut with a hacksaw rather than drilled. If you go this route, scribe parallel lines as far apart as the tang is thick, and drill a hole of what will be the closed end of the slot.

Once the slot has been cut and filed to the proper size, grind the hilt to rough, exterior dimensions. The idea is to leave as much metal as possible to work with, and thereby cover yourself should you miscalculate and get the slot slightly off center.

Should you want upswept or downswept quillons, soft metals in thicknessess up to ¼-inch can be bent easily by heating (with a propane torch) and peening while the stock is held in a vise. Even cast hilts can be bent in this manner if you take it slow and don't get carried away with your peening.

F. Remove oil and grease with acetone.
G. Clamp hilt to tang.

SOLDERING THE HILT

With slot cut and filed, quillons bent (if desired), and hilt rough ground to its approximate final shape, you're ready to solder hilt to tang. For this purpose, use *only* silver solder. This stuff is an alloy composed of about 96 percent tin and 4

H. Dribble flux into joint.

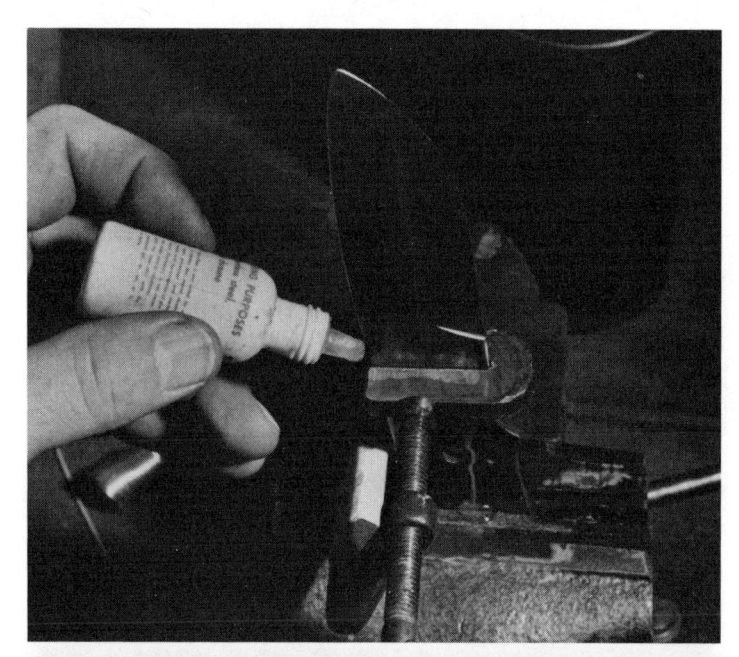

I. Heat hilt and tang from below with propane torches.

percent silver. Solder alloyed of tin and lead won't give you a strong enough bond, and it will tarnish.

Kester makes an excellent flux-core round-wire silver solder, or you can use the fusion paste-flux product favored by many gunsmiths. It's available in several formulations from Brownells. The latter product combines flux with solder in a stable paste form, and it is extremely easy to use. Kester's round-wire product is available from nearly any good hardware store or builder's supply.

Silver solder has a slightly higher melting point than common lead solder, so you will have to use a propane torch. Soldering irons and guns simply won't generate enough heat. Some silver solders have melting points that exceed or approach the temperature at which carbon steel loses its temper (around 800 degrees). Should you use one of these high-temperature solders, you'll get the best possible bond, but you *must* use a heat-control paste to protect your blade. It's easier, and safer, to use the low-temperature stuff such as Kester's, which melts at around 450-500 degrees F.

The real trick to getting a good soldering bond is to get your work super clean. The best bet is to use steel wool, followed by acetone or carbon tet

J. Apply solder and allow capillary action to fill joint. Solder will bead if metal is too hot.

to remove all traces of oil and grease. Even when using a flux-core solder, it's good to dribble a few drops of liquid zinc chloride flux on the solder area before applying the torch. This removes any oxide from the surface of your work, and helps set up the capillary action that draws the silver solder into the bonding area or joint.

As shown in the accompanying photographs, use a "C" clamp to hold the hilt in position and place the lower portion of the tang in a machinist's vise. Heat the hilt all the way around by directing the tip of your flame at the *underside* of the hilt. This causes the solder to flow into the joint by capillary action. If you have two torches, use them both—one on each side of the hilt. Only about a minute of direct heat is required if two torches are used.

If you are using a low-temperature solder, your metal is hot enough when the brass begins to take on a deeper color. Nickel silver conducts heat more slowly than brass so slightly longer heating times are required. If you use aluminum, you'll have to use a special aluminum solder or be satisfied with epoxying your hilt. I don't work with aluminum hilts for this reason.

K. Allow to cool at room temperature and remove excess solder with needle file or knife.

Never apply heat directly to the solder. Instead, bring the hilt and tang to the temperature necessary to sustain the solder in a liquid state, and apply it directly to the joint. As soon as the solder begins to flow freely, remove the flame. Thereafter, use your torch sparingly, because overheating weakens the bond.

L. Rough taper hilt with Moto-Tool.

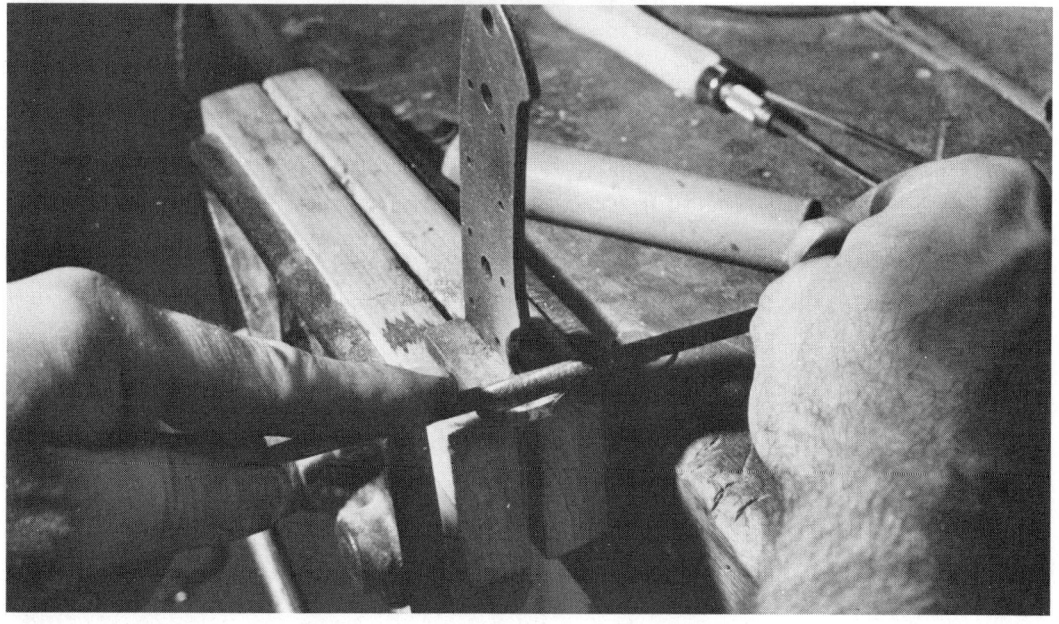

M. Complete taper with rat-tail file (final finishing will be done after slabs are attached).

Regardless of whether your pommel material is bar stock, casting, or (as shown here) antler crown, the procedure for preparing a tapped pommel (or butt cap) to fit on a round tang is essentially the same. Here are the steps you follow:
A. If tang is not pre-threaded, use file to round the upper portion of the tang.

Allow your work to cool at room temperature (never quench it) and check the joint. If there are gaps in it, start all over again by melting out the old solder and fluxing again. Reheated solder lacks bonding ability. This may cause you to shudder but whack the hilt on the top of your workbench a couple of times to be sure you have a good bond. It's a whole lot easier to resolder at this point than after you've got your handle in place.

Clean up excess solder with a needle file and 400-grit emery cloth. You can also bring your hilt to its final shape at this time, but don't get carried away. Remember, the final sanding and buffing will be done *after* the handle is on the tang.

MAKING THE POMMEL

The way you construct your pommel depends upon the type of tang you are using. As we discussed earlier, a round tang calls for a drilled and tapped pommel. A modified tang calls for a slotted and pinned pommel; a short tang usually indicates a butt plate or cap, and a full-tang is usually completed without a pommel.

If your project calls for a drilled and tapped

B. Select a dye to fit the diameter of the rounded tang, and one which has no fewer than 24 threads per inch. Use dye to cut threads in the tang.

pommel, the first step is to drill your hole in the approximate center of the stock you are working with. Do this first, *before* you begin shaping the pommel. Quarter-inch bar stock is the thinnest you can work with and get enough threads for a secure hold. Three-eighths-inch or ½-inch stock is better, and if you plan to shape your pommel into the popular overhanging-lip design, you'll likely want to work with ⅝-inch material.

Select a bit that is the appropriate diameter for the threaded tang. Most pre-threaded tangs are made to receive a standard 10 × 24 machine-screw thread, and this calls for a 9/64-inch bit. This is also a good size to work with if you are threading your own tang.

It's easier to drill a precisely perpendicular hole with a drill press, but I've been using a hand drill for years simply by securing the pommel stock in a vise and "eyeballing" it. If you're a gnat's whisker off, no one but you will know once the knife is assembled.

Affix your handle, following the procedures discussed in the next chapter, and screw the pommel into place. Be sure to use spacers between handle and pommel.

Now, with handle and pommel firmly in

place, saw and grind the pommel into shape and finish it as you do the handle. You will probably find it necessary to make some adjustments, such as grinding off a fraction of an inch of the threaded tang, before you obtain perfect fit. All this work should be done, and perfect alignment achieved,

C. Using a bit of the same diameter as the tang, drill a perfectly centered hole in the pommel. Note masking tape on bit to assure that blind hole is drilled no deeper than necessary.

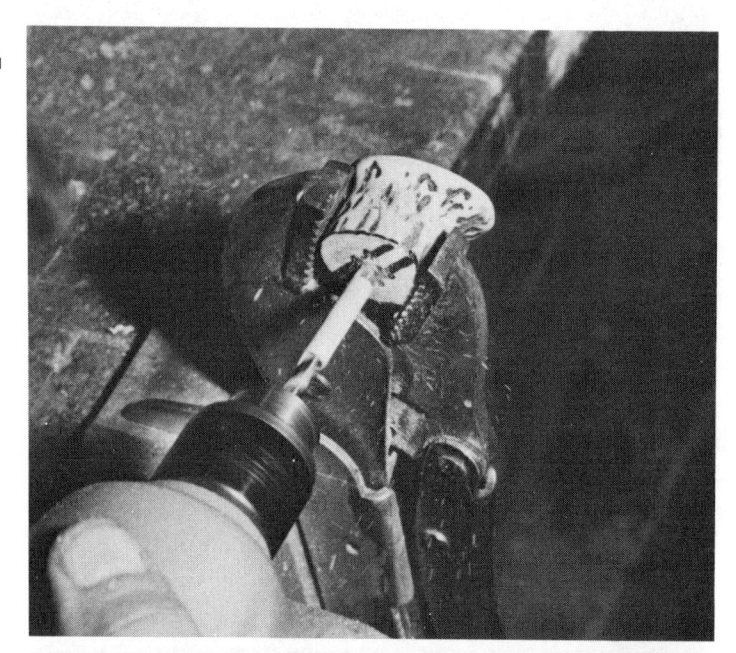

D. Using a tap of the same diameter and thread size as the dye used to thread the tang, cut threads in the blind hole just drilled.

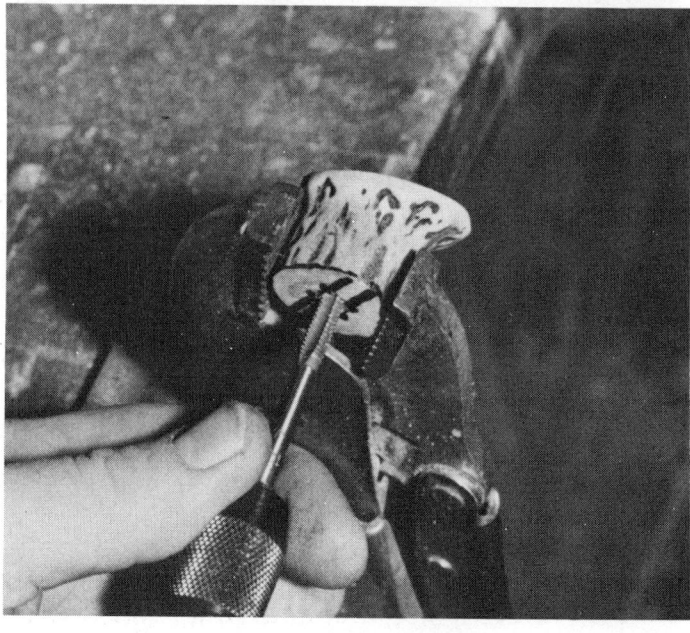

before you begin your final grinding. Use epoxy when you secure your pommel the final time.

If the tang you are working with is of modified design, the approach you take will differ somewhat. Instead of a threaded hole, you will want a blind slot in the pommel. Proceed pretty much as you did when you slotted your hilt, only this time don't drill all the way through. Because you must have enough room for a pin, you will have to work with stock that's at least ½-inch thick. The slot itself should be about ⅜-inch deep.

If you have a Moto-Tool, it's a snap to finish the sides of the slot using Dremel's 9901 or 9902 tungsten carbide cutters. A flat needle file works as well but takes a little longer.

With the slot prepared, use a square to scribe a line at precisely a right angle to the slot. Use a center punch to mark a spot 3/16-inch from the bottom (toward the handle) of the pommel, and drill a hole using a 5/64-inch drill bit. This will precisely accommodate a pin made from 10-gauge copper wire. With the hole drilled all the way through the pommel, insert the tang into the slot and use a small punch or bit to mark the place on the tang where you want to drill out the pin hole. Remove the tang, then drill a 5/64-inch hole.

E. Using a file (if metal) or a rasp (if wood or bone), square the end of the pommel so that it aligns perfectly with the handle.

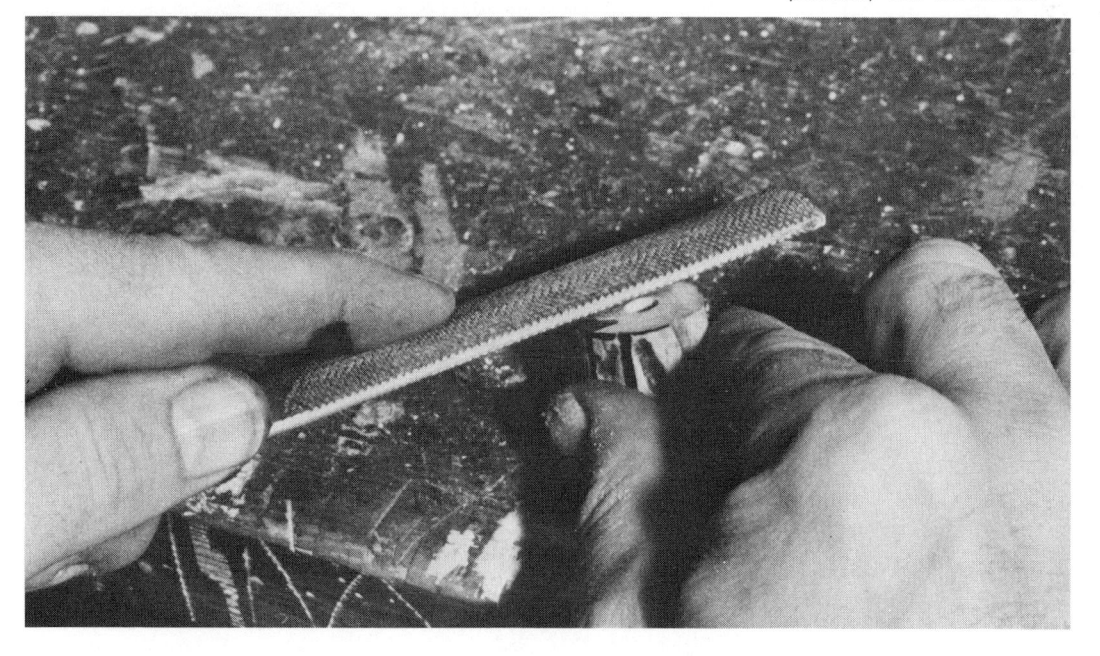

With handle and spacers in place, coat the end of the tang with epoxy and insert it in the slot. Insert a sharpened pin, about a ¼-inch longer than the pommel is wide, into the hole and drive it through. Clip the pin about 1/16-inch above the pommel on each side. Allow the epoxy to cure, then place the pinned pommel on a piece of flat steel and peen the pin until it is almost flush with the pommel. This will cause the soft copper wire to swell and grip both pommel and tang, giving a solid fit. From here, proceed to grind and sand pommel and handle to shape.

Many times, a short tang is used and no pommel or butt cap is desired, as with a stag crown. However, affixing a pommel is a simple matter, and your options are greater than with

F. Dribble full-strength epoxy into the tapped pommel hole.

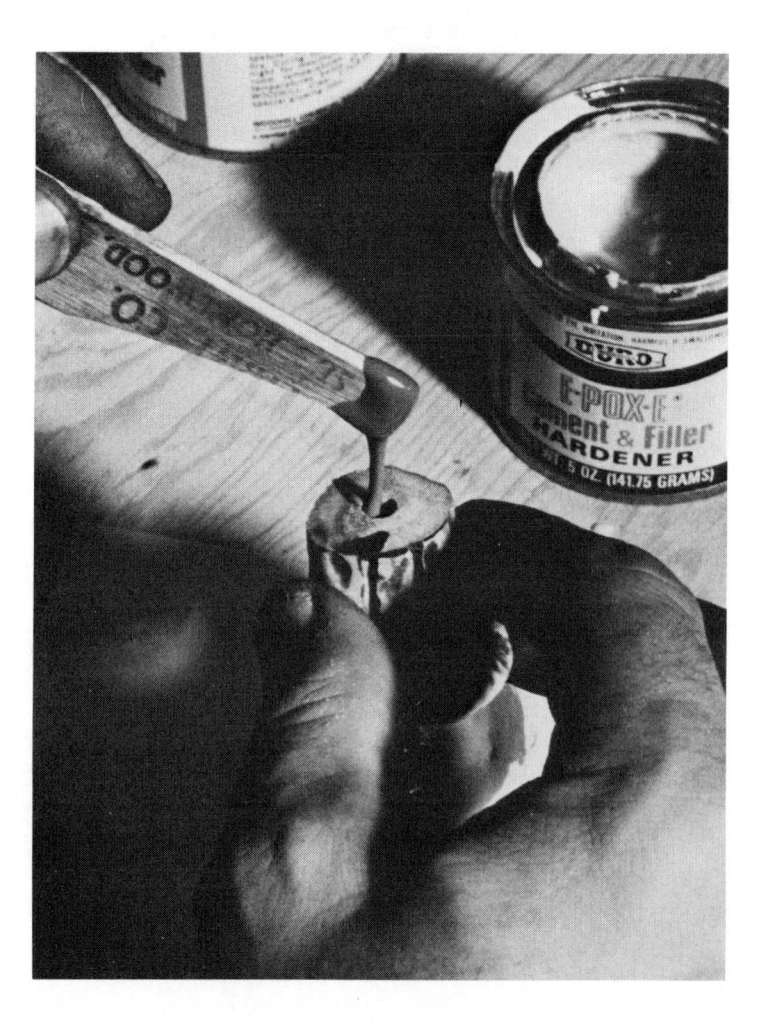

either the round or modified tang. This time, instead of making a threaded hole or blind slot in the pommel, you will want to silver solder a *brass* flat-head screw to the pommel or cap.

Begin by drilling a shallow (1/16-inch is plenty) hole in the pommel stock that is large enough to accept the head of the screw. Place the stock in a vise and heat it with a propane torch until it reaches solder-melting temperature. Melt a few drops of solder in the blind hole, and (using vise grips or pliers), set the head of the screw in the hole. Continue to hold your torch on the pommel and add a few more drops of silver solder around the screw head. Allow to cool at room temperature.

While the pommel is cooling, drill a hole in the top of the handle large enough to accept the screw. Countersink it slightly. Cut spacers to fit and slip them over the screw. Epoxy and tighten, then finish handle and pommel together.

This method of assembly has the advantage of allowing you to work with just about any thickness of pommel or butt cap stock desired, down to 1/8-inch or less. This is also a good method to use for affixing pommels made from stag crowns or

G. With handle and spacers in place, coat the tang with additional epoxy and screw the pommel into place. Allow epoxy to cure before proceeding further.

other nonmetallic material. Instead of silver-soldering a brass screw in place (as with metal), you use a double-threaded screw and drill holes in both the pommel and handle. Double-threaded screws are more commonly used to mount ceiling hangers for swag lamps and such. Every hardware store carries them.

There's one last pommel design that I want to mention. I guess I've got to take credit (or blame) for it, because I haven't seen others like it.

Working with 3/32-inch aluminum stock, laminate three pieces of aluminum with an equal number of pieces of black spacer material. Epoxy these together, and then pin them to the handle with sharpened copper or aluminum pin. This method of construction is both lightweight and attractive, and works equally well with round-tang or short-tang design. The photo and illustration show better what I mean than words can describe.

Pinned and laminated pommel

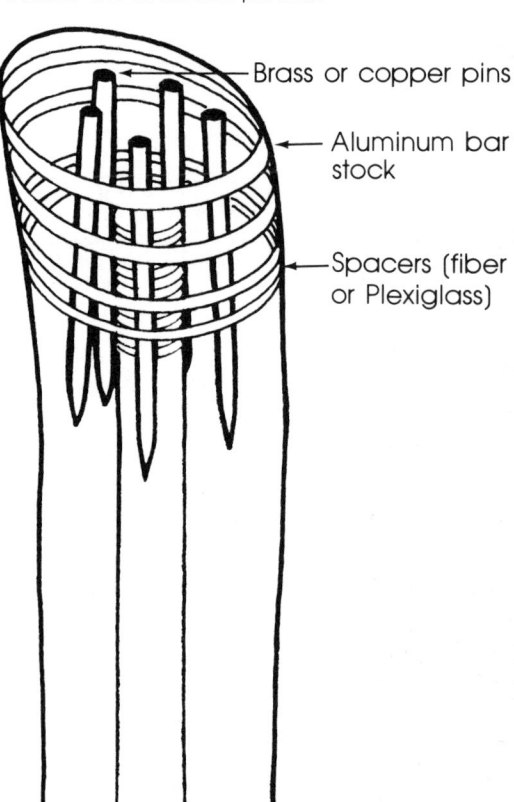

- Brass or copper pins
- Aluminum bar stock
- Spacers (fiber or Plexiglass)

CHAPTER 11

THE HANDLE: An Expression of Your Individuality

Making the handle for your knife is where individuality really comes into its own. Working with wood, leather, synthetics, buffalo horn, stag, or any one of several other materials, you can make your handle just as plain or fancy as you want.

However, lest your fancy fly too high, keep in mind that a knife is a tool, and the only real function of the handle is to give your paw something to hang onto while you use it. Maybe it would be worth our while to examine that thought a little further:

Remember our earlier mention of the deerfoot handles that presumably were popular back around the turn of the century. Today such handles are viewed as curiosity pieces by collectors, and with disdain by most outdoorsmen. Yet some of today's custom knife-makers, trying I suppose to please the fetishes of their wealthy customers, are cranking out stuff that's almost as bad. I saw one photo of a knife with—would you believe—a bear's jaw and teeth intact.

In my book it's the blade, not the handle, that's supposed to do the damage. Just remember, whenever you start dolling up your handle to make it more attractive, there's a pretty good chance that you are going to sacrifice something in the way of practicality. For most of us, the best design lies somewhere between fancy enough to give pride of authorship and simple enough to be practical.

With that out of the way, let's turn our attention to some of the more usual materials you'll likely be working with as you design and shape your handle.

THE SYNTHETICS

Man, in his boundless quest for something that does the job better than nature's own materials, has developed, through chemistry, all sorts of plastic and synthetic materials. A lot of these—perhaps too many—have been used for knife handles. Some undoubtedly are good: Delrin used by Buck, Frontier, and other manufacturers. Ivoryite used by Randall Knives. Micarta used by many customizers and generally considered today's "wonder" material. Because the latter is so widely used, it's worth closer attention.

Micarta is made by impregnating wood laminate, linen, or paper with a phenolic resin. The process was developed by Westinghouse, and the name is trademarked by them. It takes a lot of abuse, works well with sanders and routers, and buffs to a high luster. But it has some drawbacks too.

Bone or ivory-colored Micarta, in particular, is difficult to work with because it almost always contains tiny imperfections that can mar the beauty of the finished handle. Just about the time you think you've got your handle polished to perfection, a black speck or two will appear, and back to the emery cloth you must go. It also will turn yellowish under high-speed buffing. You'll find that most professional knife-makers will charge $10 or $15 extra for ivory Micarta, and this is why.

Micarta comes in three other colors, to my

knowledge: a black that resembles ebony, a dark tan that resembles walnut, and a reddish brown that resembles rosewood. These varieties have tiny imperfections too, but because of their darker color the specks aren't as visible.

Because it is a laminate, Micarta will split. This is either good or bad, depending on how you look at it. On the plus side, it's a snap to convert Micarta blocks to scales, because one good tap with a wood chisel will split it right down the middle. On the negative side, don't push your drill bit too hard, or start it with center punch, or you're apt to have scales whether you want them or not.

Micarta in all four color variations is priced competitively with the exotic hardwoods, and it is available through the supply houses listed in the appendix.

Drilling a perfectly straight hole through the block or stick is the most critical part of wooden handle construction. Here are the steps to follow:

A. Use a soft pencil and square to mark guidelines on each dimension of the block—length, width, and both ends.

THE HARDWOODS

Just about every species of hardwood has been used for handle-making material over the years. Beech is still a great favorite of the fishing-knife and kitchen-knife manufacturers, and you'll still see hickory used to some extent. Of the common

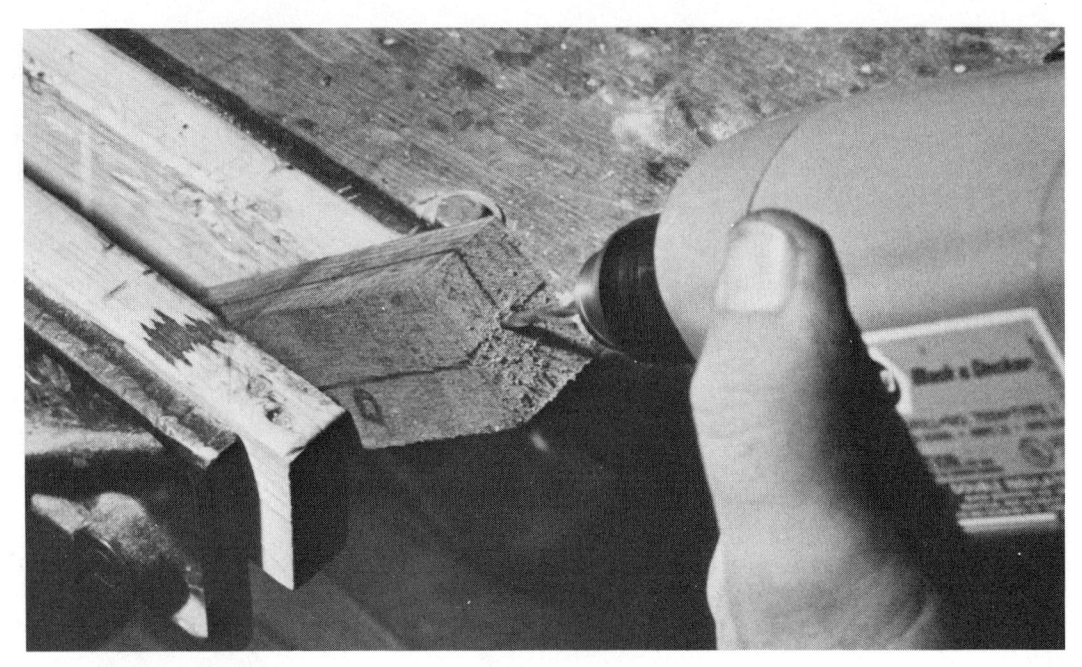

B. Use a small (approx. 3/16-inch) bit to drill guide holes in each end of the wooden block (or antler). Sight down the penciled guidelines you have drawn to maintain both horizontal and vertical control.

cabinet woods, walnut, mahogany, and hard maple are marginally acceptable as handle stock, if you dress them with a good filler and sealer. Tulip, myrtle, basswood, and mesquite also have some value, but not much. Nearly all the American woods are either too soft, too hard to work because of interlocking grain or too easily split.

For real satisfaction in your handle-making efforts, turn to the exotic imported woods from the equatorial countries. The main key to good handle stock lies in its density, and the African, Indian, and South American woods have it all over anything we grow here at home. Sorry about that, Mr. Pinchot.

Here is my list, which I don't claim to be comprehensive, of some of the better exotic woods being used by knife-makers today:

Ebony — An extremely dark, fine-grained wood that has been used for knife-making for more than a century. It polishes well without oiling or other finish, but its propensity for splitting makes it difficult to work with and less than desirable in a finished handle. Unless you're a stickler for authenticity, I'd suggest avoiding it.

C. With guide holes drilled from each end, follow the same procedure with wood bit of approximately the same diameter as the tang is wide. Hole can be enlarged or straightened with small round rasp if necessary. Block will now be rough sanded or sawn to size, and epoxied or fiberglassed to the tang at the time the pommel is screwed into place.

African Blackwood — As dark as ebony and extremely fine-grained and dense. Polished, it takes a deep satin finish, and it doesn't split like ebony. Sad to say, it's in short supply and about twice as expensive as most other exotics.

Cocobolo — Fine-grained and durable, this is a favorite of knife-makers and pistol smiths alike. It's used by Smith & Wesson for their magnum grips. Lighter in color than rosewood, it has streaks running from dark brown to black throughout. It can be oiled, but takes a nice semi-lustrous finish without it.

Bocote — This African import has alternating bands of yellow and brown, interspersed with narrower stripes of black. It takes a good luster on buffing, but tends to darken with age. It is fairly resinous and doesn't require oiling.

Difou — Usually called "golden pheasant" in the trade, this has a pale golden color and a nice firm grain. It's extremely hard and takes a beautiful finish. An unusual effect can be obtained by scorching with a propane torch to get alternating bands of reddish-bronze color. It's hard to work, but worth the effort.

Lauro — Ranges in color from dark walnut to light cream, with bands of light purple to black. It's an easy wood to work and takes a good, but not particularly lustrous finish. Oiling accents its color and grain.

LaPacho — Sometimes spelled with a "U" after the "A" (Paucho), this South American import is about the color of walnut and almost without figure. It works extremely well, and is a good choice if you plan to score or checker your handle. It buffs well and requires no filler, but an oil finish will add to its luster.

Lignum Vitae — Another South American import, this is so dense it refuses to float. It has a straight yellow-and-brown striped figure and buffs to a high gloss. It's hard to work (use a sharp drill bit) but gives an extremely durable handle. Don't use it if you want a lightweight knife.

Rosewood — This old favorite of the gunstock maker (for accent pieces) has one of the most pleasing grains and colors of any wood. Oiled and polished, it takes on a deep purplish color; not as dark as ebony, but with more contrast. It works well and takes a high luster.

Zebrawood — As the name implies, this is a heavily figured wood with alternating bands of light tan to light cream, interspersed with black. It works as easily as walnut and buffs to a nice luster. Oil finishing accents the figure.

LEATHER

Time was when leather handles were about the only kind you could get in a store-bought sheath knife. Its disadvantages have caused it to lose favor in recent years, however; it tends to shrink and mildew unless properly cared for.

Leather handles are made, of course, by cutting and laminating discs or washers cut from heavy cowhide. You can cut your own from 12-oz hide, or buy them pre-cut and slotted for about 20 cents each. The average-size knife handle requires about 16 to 18 washers cut from 12-oz hide. The ones you buy are made from thicker stuff and only about 14 are required.

The washers are slipped over a round tang one at a time, and glued together using a rubber-base contact cement. Then the handle is finished pretty much as you would other material by shaping on a sanding disc and with rasps. Buff to polish and treat with a leather preservative.

I've cut and slotted my own washers just to see if I could, but it's hardly worth the effort when you can buy pre-cut ones so cheaply. I've found that a wood chisel is the most practical way of cutting and slotting.

A. The components that will be used to build a knife using leather-disc handle construction and antler-crown pommel are laid out.

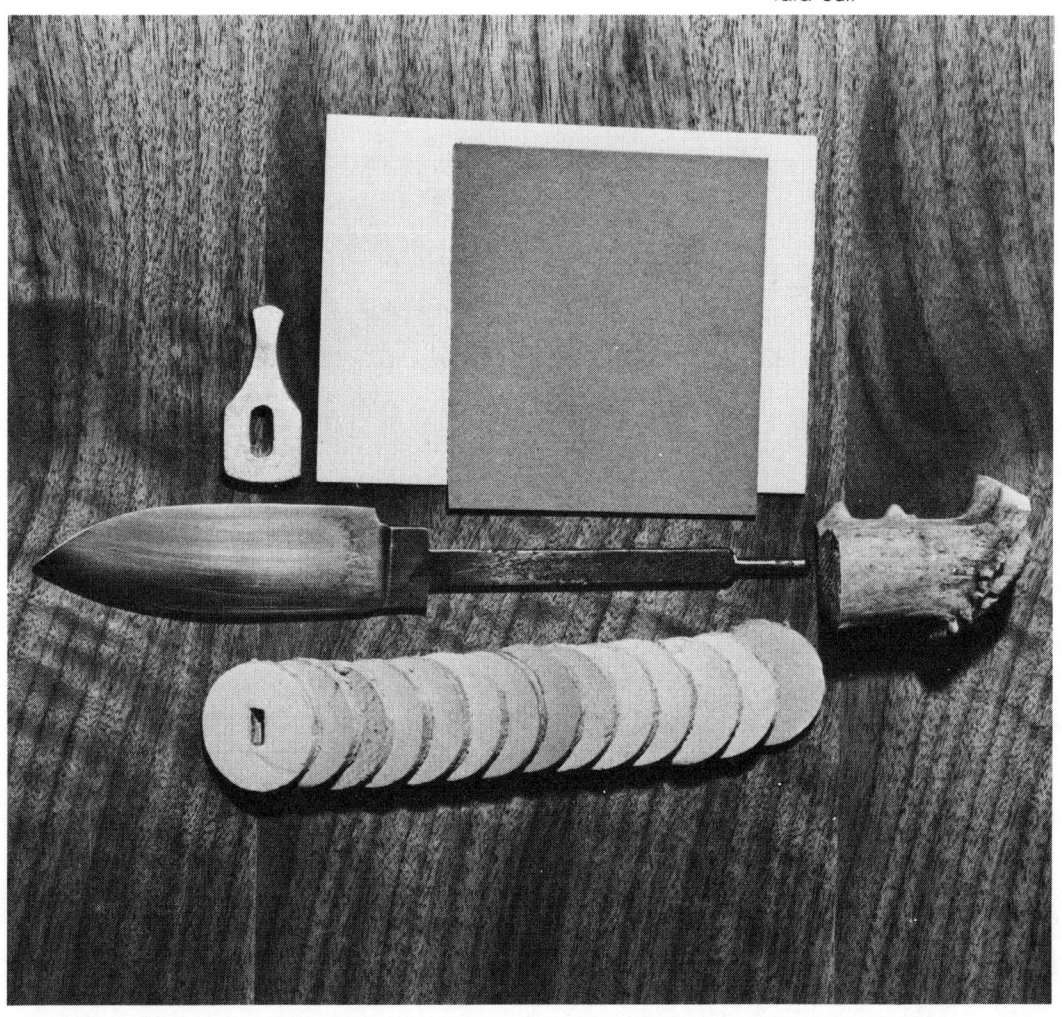

B. Spacers are fitted onto the tang and epoxied into place.

C. Leather discs are sanded briefly to roughen them prior to cemeting.

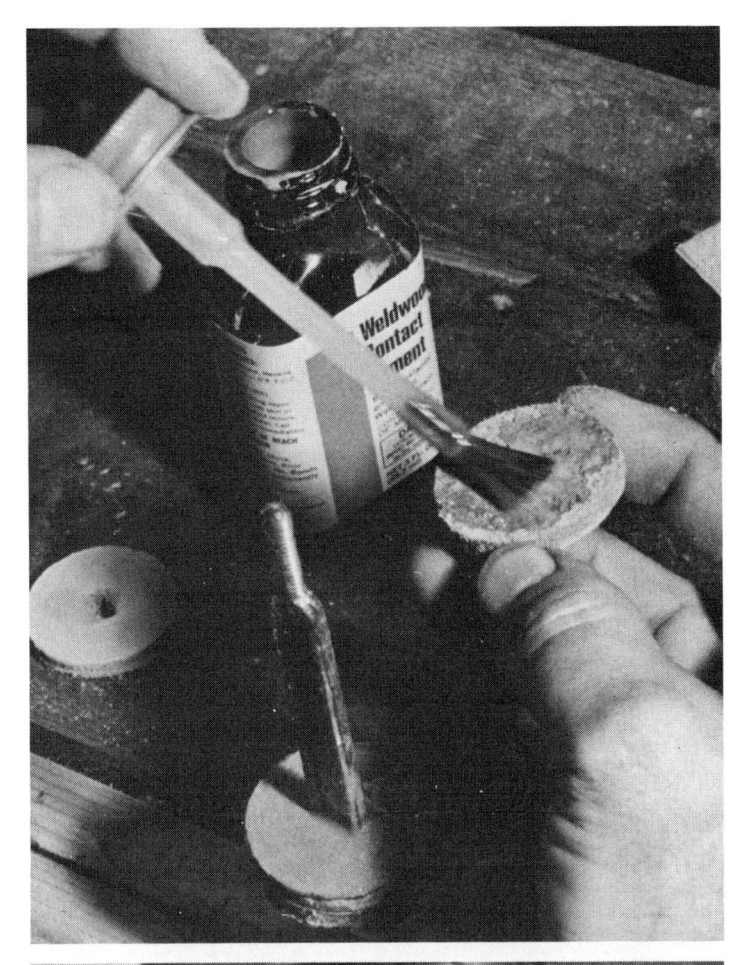

D. Contact cement is spread on both surfaces to be joined.

E. Mallet and dowel are used to tap discs lightly and assure uniform fit.

F. Pommel spacers are added and epoxied in place.

G. With pommel and handle cemented and secured, leather handle is shaped on rotary sanding disc.

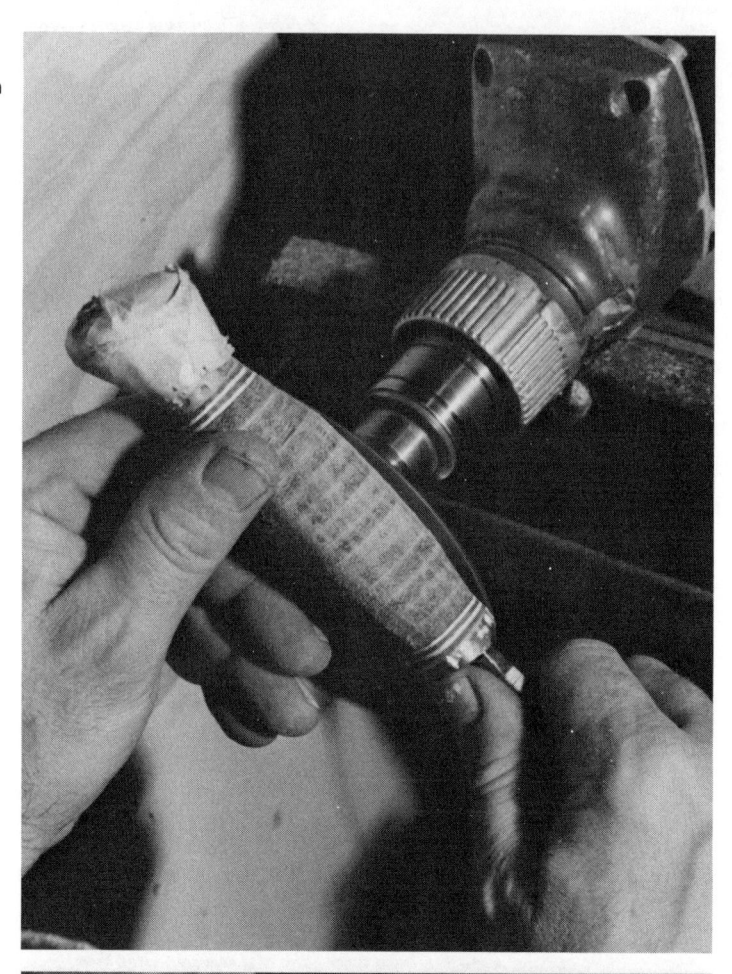

H. Finger cutouts are added with round rasp or Moto-Tool.

HORN AND STAG

My experience with buffalo horn is fairly limited; I probably wouldn't have used it at all if E. Christopher Firearms Co. hadn't thrown a couple of scales in with some other stuff I'd ordered. The stuff I used is black with some white streaks, but I understand that solid black is more common.

I also have a kris that a friend brought me from Singapore that uses a brown material he tells me is buffalo horn for the sash piece. So I assume the material can be had in brown as well as black. In my limited experience, horn drills, inlets, and sands easily, and polishes to a deep, mirrorlike finish.

What we call "stag" is the antler material from elk, deer, caribou, or moose. Practically all of the commercially available stag comes from a large (nearly as big as our elk) Indian deer known as the sambar. Watching a television program about the migration of the barren-land caribou recently, I was given to wonder why some enterprising soul doesn't pick up shed antlers from their Arctic calving grounds. But as far as I know, such a market has never been established.

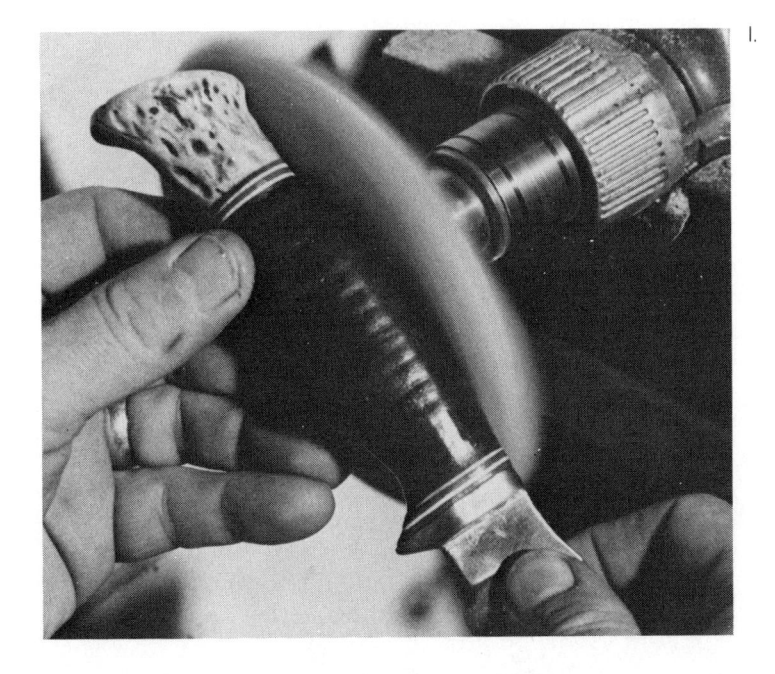

1. Handle is buffed and polished for final finish.

Knife handles I've seen made from moose antlers are finished to a smooth bone appearance, so its use as traditional rough-finished stag is apparently limited by its size and configuration. One of these days, I want to try working with it, but haven't yet had the opportunity.

Most of my experience in working with stag has been using antlers from the white-tailed deer. It has long been my favorite handle stock, and I see no good reason to change my opinion at this late date. I've worked also with mule deer and elk antlers, and of course with sambar stag. I think my bias for whitetail antlers has something to do with nostalgia, plus the fact that it was my buddies or I who have brought to bag all the deer which provided them.

I've found that there *is* a difference in coloration of whitetail antlers. In my experience, antlers taken from eastern bucks usually finish grey, while those from western animals finish to a much more pleasing white. I assume it has something to do with diet.

If you want deep relief in your stag handle, you're better off buying sambar stock. Because these deer are much larger than those we grow at

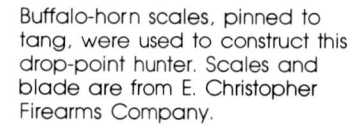

Buffalo-horn scales, pinned to tang, were used to construct this drop-point hunter. Scales and blade are from E. Christopher Firearms Company.

home, their antlers are bigger, straighter, and more deeply etched. Although the better suppliers try to match up their scales, getting two from the same antler is pure luck. If you want perfectly matched scales, you'll do better to buy it as a stick and saw it yourself. This is easily done with a backsaw if you take your time.

Let me mention, before moving on to the next subject, that fallen antlers are fine if you happen onto them within a few months after they are dropped. Otherwise, the decaying process has begun and the antlers have developed too much porosity to make good handle stock.

ETCHING STAG

One of the more attractive methods of producing a knife handle from stag is to use the natural base, or crown, as the pommel. Deer, regardless of species, have an annoying habit of growing small basal tines on their antlers, and these, of course, must be removed if the crown is to have utilitarian value. When the basal tine is removed and sanded, this leaves an area that interferes with the usual deep-relief pattern of the rest of the stick.

If you, like me, find this undesirable, you can overcome it by etching false relief lines in the cutaway area. This is done most easily using a Moto-Tool and small carving cutter. It can also be done with a flexible shaft attached to your bench-mounted hand drill. Dremel's cutting tip (which can be purchased separately) works well here also or you can make a serviceable etching tool by flat-grinding the tip of a small drill bit.

When you have etched relief lines that match the length and depth of the rest of the stick, coat the whole thing with a dark oil-base stain or burnt umber and let it dry. Then, return to your sander and remove all the stain from the raised surfaces. The relief lines, both real and artificial, retain their characteristic deep brown color, and the raised areas are finished in a nicely contrasting white.

I've had experts look at handles finished this

way without tumbling to how it's done. One friendly critic, who's also into knife-making, even came over to the house and had me *prove* to him that the method works. Now he's doing it himself.

CONSTRUCTING YOUR HANDLE

The step-by-step photos accompanying this chapter will, I believe, show you how to construct and finish your handle better than words. So I'll cover it only briefly in the text.

To some extent, the type of tang you are working with will determine the design of your handle, and the construction method you follow. Generally speaking, round tangs call for blocks or sticks, and full tangs call for slabs or scales. A crown or sharply curving stick usually calls for a shortened tang, and a fully enclosed (modified) tang means that you will want to inlet your scales.

These are very general observations, and you will find yourself altering construction methods in an infinite number of ways. I've frequently, for example, used scales with round tangs and inlet the area occupied by the tang. I'm convinced that

Steps to follow in inletting scales (full-tang construction):
A. Using graph paper, trace outline of blade and tang.

with modern epoxies this method is just about as strong as a solid stick, but you can also use pins if you're so inclined.

One thing you want to be very sure of when you're working with scales is that the inner surfaces are smooth and match up perfectly. Spend some time making certain that yours are and do;

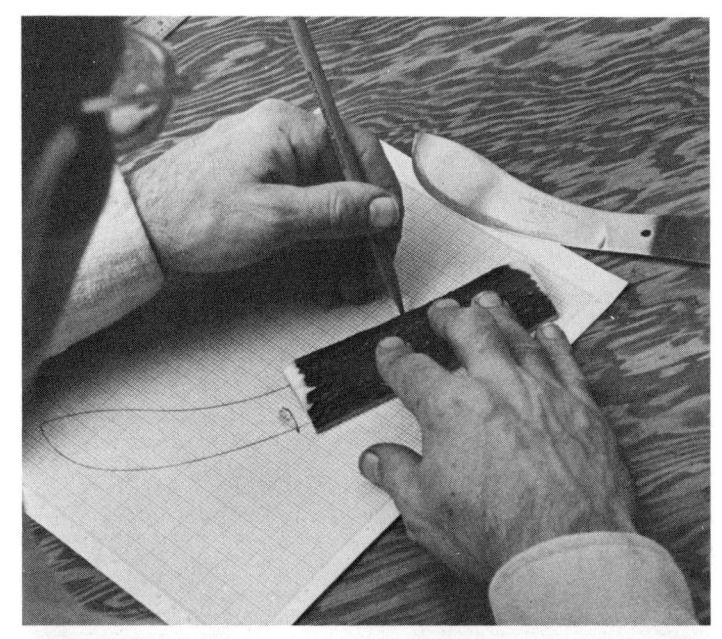

B. Place scale over tang and trace its outline.

C. Sketch design of finished handle; if tang is too large to accommodate design, grinding will be required.

otherwise you'll wind up with a most unprofessional job and an unsightly epoxy line.

Some knife-makers seem to prefer to do almost all their handle-shaping after their knives are completely assembled. My preference is to get all the rough work out of the way ahead of time, then complete the final touches, such as finger cutouts, after the knife is put together.

D. Transfer outline of tang to scale.

E. Use felt-tip marker to outline tang-area to be inlet.

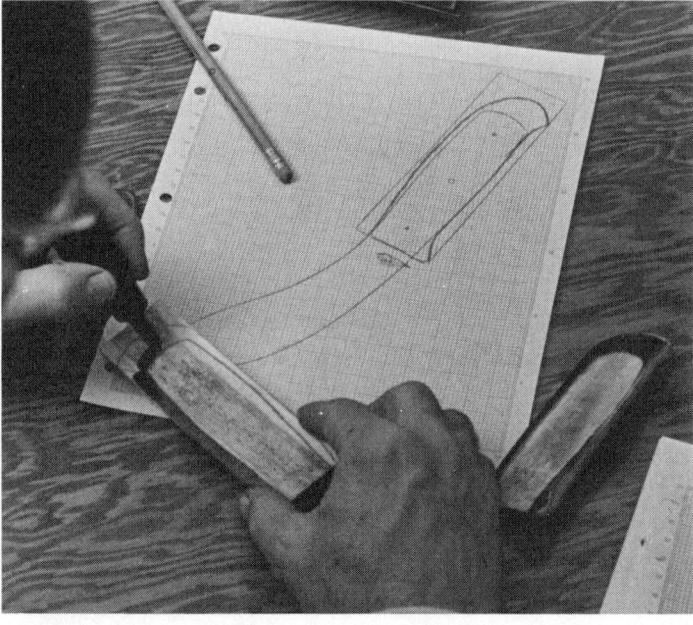

MAKING THE HANDLE FIT YOUR HAND

One of the best parts about making your own knife is that you can shape its handle to fit your hand. It's sort of like having a custom-made gunstock. It's always good to begin your handle design on a piece of graph paper.

I do this by tracing the outline of the blade and tang, then drawing in freehand the configuration that I want my hilt, handle, and pommel to have when I get through. I place my hand, palm down, on the paper and mark where it will go on the handle. With this as my guide, I doodle back and forth until I have a handle that seems to fit.

I won't say this is essential, and sometimes the material (such as a stag crown) you're working with is the most decisive factor. Still, it's mighty comforting to have something to look at when you're about halfway through your shaping and wondering what to do next. Moreover, drawing a pattern forces you to anticipate construction problems in advance.

We've mentioned finger cutouts, and I think a further word about them is in order. I like cutouts, and use them fairly often. But they're not as prac-

F. Match scales visually to make certain dimensions are approximately the same.

G. Using Moto-Tool and inletting burr, inlet scale to one-half thickness of tang; do same on other scale.
H. Close-up of inletting burr (carving cutter) used with Moto-Tool. Other shapes and sizes are available.
I. Smooth inlet surface with flat emery wheel.

tical as some folks would have you believe. The whole idea behind cutouts is to give you better control of your blade, and keep the cutting edge headed in the right direction. But consider, if you will, that a skinning blade is used with the edge up about as much as with the edge down, which means that the cutouts are going to be facing into your palm about half the time.

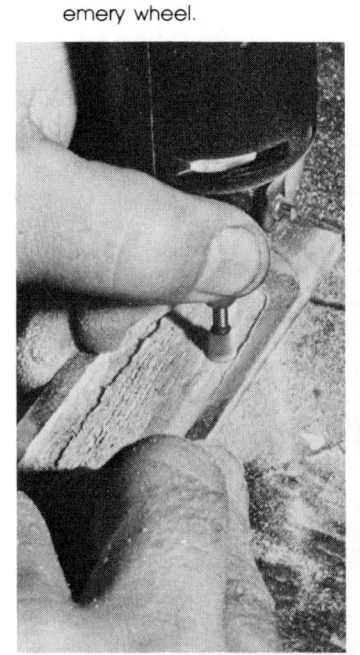

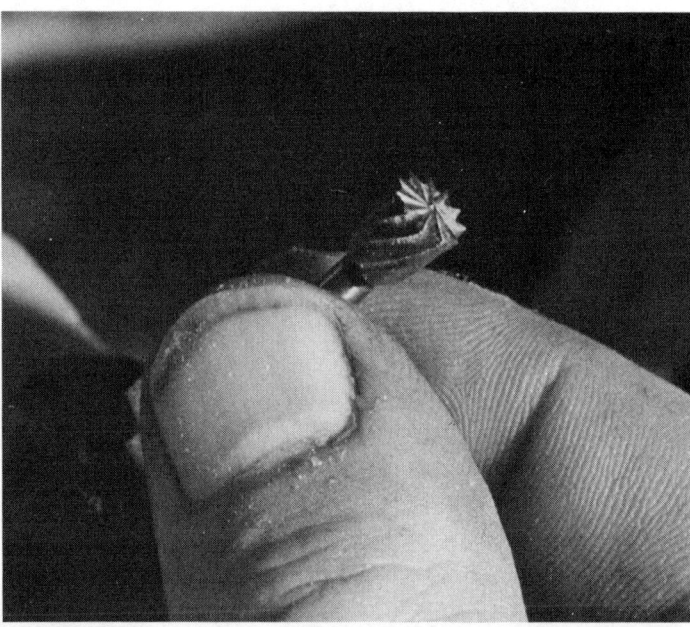

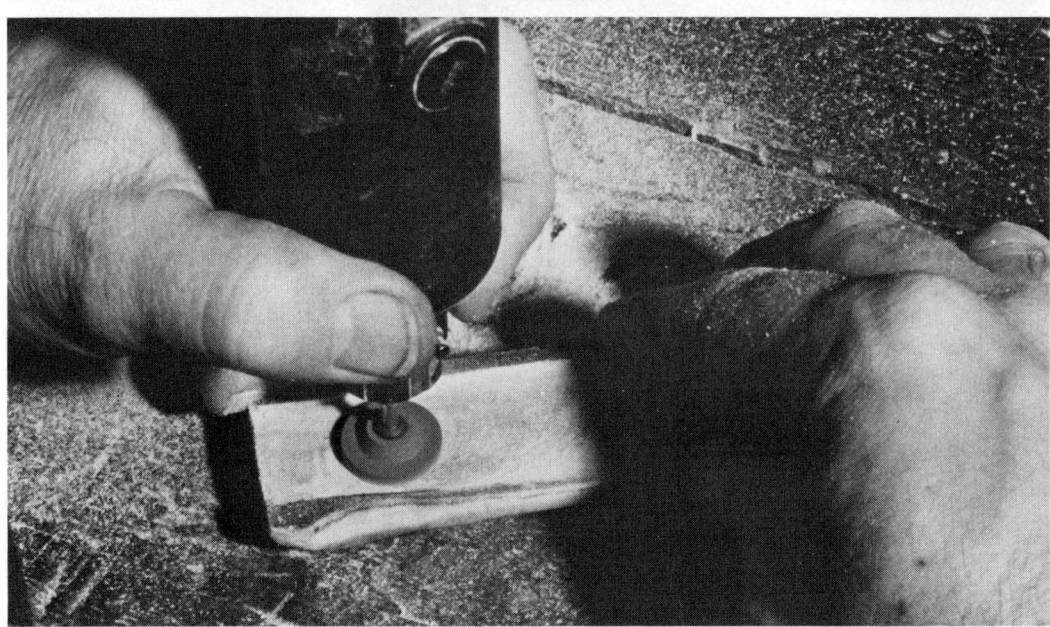

If the cutouts are fairly shallow, this presents no real problem. But some of the custom designs I've seen cutouts that resemble Pike's Peak, and I can't see how the owners use them for anything other than hanging on the wall.

I'm bothered too, by the way some—make that *most*—knife handles are contoured today. If you close your fist, you'll see that the largest part of your palm is in the middle, the next-to-largest part is up by your thumb, and the smallest part is down where your little finger closes. Yet how many handles do you see that are designed with this in mind?

I've done a fair amount of experimenting, and concluded that the tip, not the base, of a deer antler—with a single finger cutout near the hilt—comes as close as any to being the perfect handle design. Now this might rank as fairly momentous news, were it not for one small fact: Bill Scagel knew that more than 70 years ago, and his knives are still around to prove it.

That's one of the problems with history. You keep rediscovering it and finding out you're not as smart as you thought you were.

J. As you progress, check fit at frequent intervals.
K. Fit both scales over tang and be sure no gaps exist; you are now ready to epoxy and drill holes for rivets or pins.

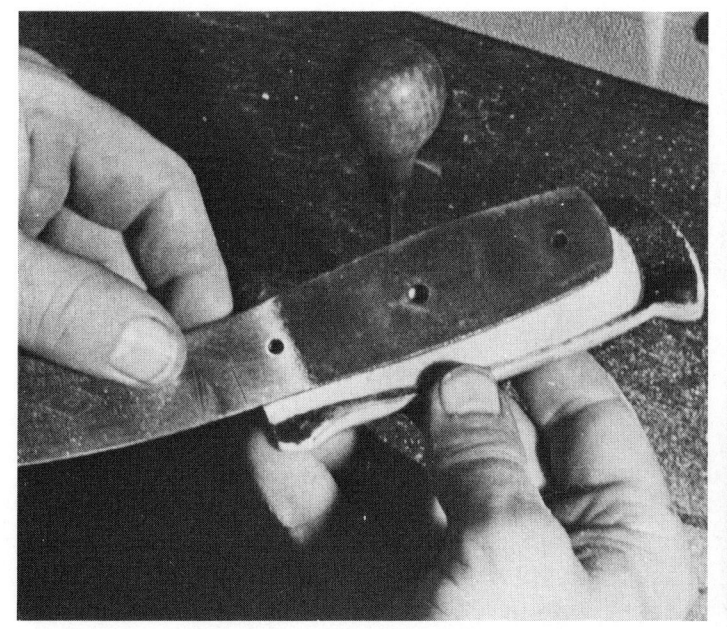

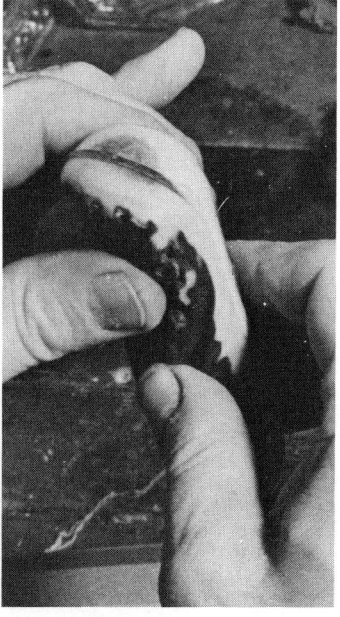

CHAPTER 12

EPOXY AND HOW TO USE IT

It's not the sort of thing a guy likes to go around admitting to just everyone, but most of my failures with epoxy have been because I (1) used stuff that has been sitting on the shelf too long, (2) didn't follow instructions, or (3) failed to keep my work area clean. Seldom has it been the fault of the product itself.

Because my sins may be yours, let's view them dispassionately one at a time. First, let it be known that epoxy ages. I don't know exactly what the shelf life is, but I suspect it's not much more than six months, and certainly under a year. Once you open it, it begins to age, and once it ages it won't bond properly.

To be on the safe side, I buy my epoxy in small amounts, and toss it out six months after I open it if it hasn't been used up. I figure that the stuff I waste that way is more than offset by not having to redo jobs.

Epoxy is simple to mix; most of it calls for equal parts of resin and hardener. Where I have usually gone wrong in the instruction-following department is getting impatient and not allowing enough curing time. If the label says it cures in three or four hours, don't try to push it and wait only two. Better to be safe, and wait six or eight hours.

On the other hand for light work there are some good 5-minute epoxys on the market, and if you wait longer than that, it won't bond. The nature of epoxys makes curing time critical; so we best observe it.

I suspect my major downfall has been in not

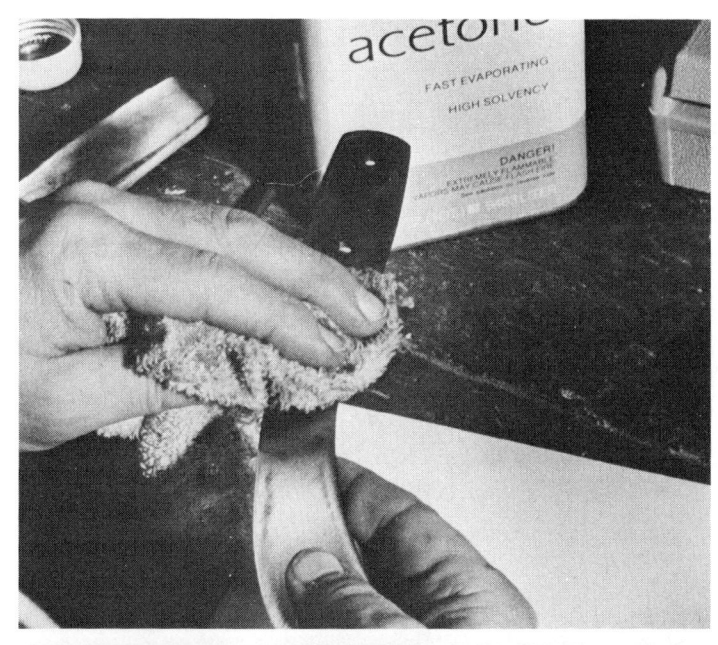

Steps to follow in using epoxy:
A. Clean all parts thoroughly with acetone or carbon tet to remove all traces of dirt, oil, and grease.

B. Mix epoxy per manufacturer's instructions; most formulations call for equal parts of resin and hardener. Mix on clean surface, such as a sheet of typing paper.

properly cleaning the surfaces to be joined or in using a mixing surface where there was a little dust or grease. Acetone is the best solvent I know to properly clean surfaces prior to using epoxy. Your usual solvents, such as naphtha-base products, are themselves oily and won't work. Use acetone also to clean up after epoxy jobs.

WHAT IT IS AND HOW IT WORKS

The epoxys in general use today are an outgrowth of technology developed during and after World War II for joining defense and industrial materials. The state of the art has now progressed to the point that epoxys have replaced conventional wood-and-metal-joining techniques for hundreds of commercial applications.

All epoxys come as two compounds, the resin itself and a hardener that is usually mixed in equal parts to cause the resin to harden. Once mixed, it can't be used again. This fact suggests a cautionary note: When using epoxy that comes in cans, use different spatulas for extracting it. A little hardener in with the resin, or vice-versa, and you've possibly spoiled the whole can.

C. Apply epoxy liberally to the parts to be bonded.

Epoxys get their joining ability from the spontaneous polymerization of resins in which an oxygen atom is combined with other connecting atoms. Thus, unlike glues, a chemical reaction occurs. The most commonly used resins are the polymides and the amines.

WHAT BRAND TO BUY?

Some of the knife-making supply houses refuse to carry epoxy because of its relatively short shelf life. Those that do usually refer to it as "commercial strength" or some such designation. In my experience I've never been able to detect a whole lot of difference between the so-called commercial stuff and that which I buy off the shelf at my local hardware store.

The folks that make it can sue me for slander if they like, but the only consistent failures (when I did my part) I've had have been with Scotch brand epoxy. If you use it, do so at your own risk.

On the other hand, I've had good luck with the Duro brand made by Woodhill Chemical Sales Corp. of Cleveland. It's my understanding that these people also sell a lot of epoxy for commer-

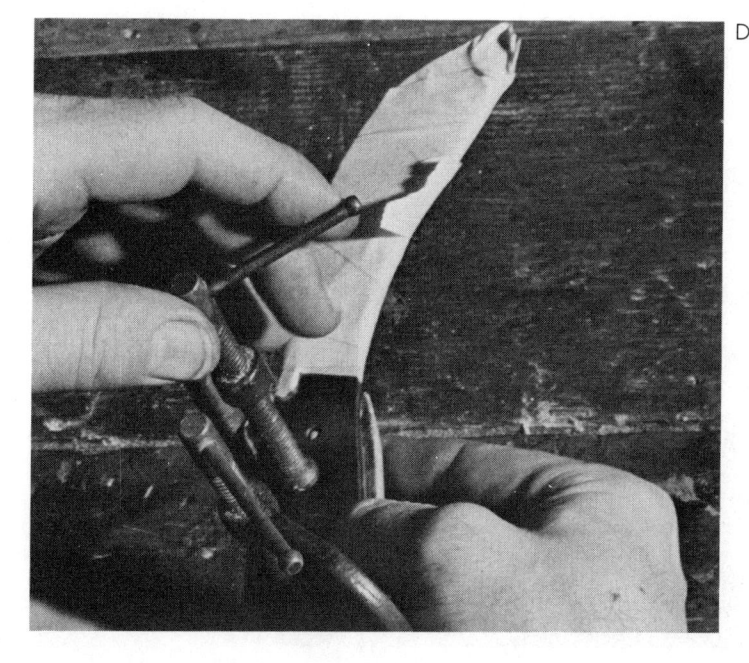

D. Clamp in position and allow to cure for the prescribed length of time; if in doubt, wait longer than manufacturer recommends.

cial applications, which perhaps accounts for the superior nature of their household line.

Duro is available in two basic formulations, both of which I've found useful. One of them is a clear liquid product, sold by the tube. You can get a variety that cures in five minutes, or one that requires 30 or 40 minutes. Their strengths, according to the tests I've made, are about equal.

Duro's other formulation has a pastelike consistency and cures in about four hours. Sold in small cans, this product is stronger than their clear liquid product, but not quite as convenient. I use it almost exclusively for bonding slabs, and have never had a failure when used correctly.

I use the clear stuff for less crucial jobs, such as bonding spacers in round tang construction. It serves its purpose equally well.

HOW TO USE EPOXYS

By pointing to the failures I've experienced, I think I've pretty well pointed you in the direction of how epoxy *should* be used. Mix it thoroughly on a completely clean surface (a clean sheet of bond paper is excellent), follow instructions, and get it

Steps to follow in using fiberglass resin for round-tang and short-tang construction:
A. Fiberglass is cut or chopped into small pieces, about one-half inch in length.

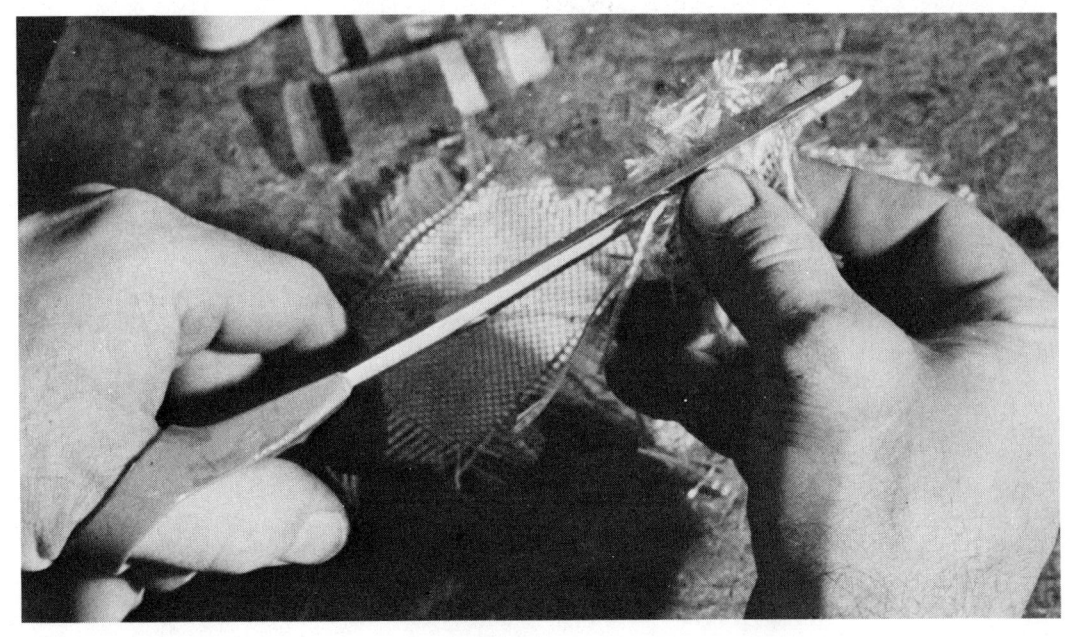

into every corner. Clamp the parts with moderate pressure, and don't worry if some oozes out. This can be sanded off later.

Another epoxy material, which I like to use with round and short tangs, is fiberglass resin. Here also, I've been happy with the Duro brand.

What you do here is chop up the fiberglass into short (½-inch or so) pieces, mix it in with the

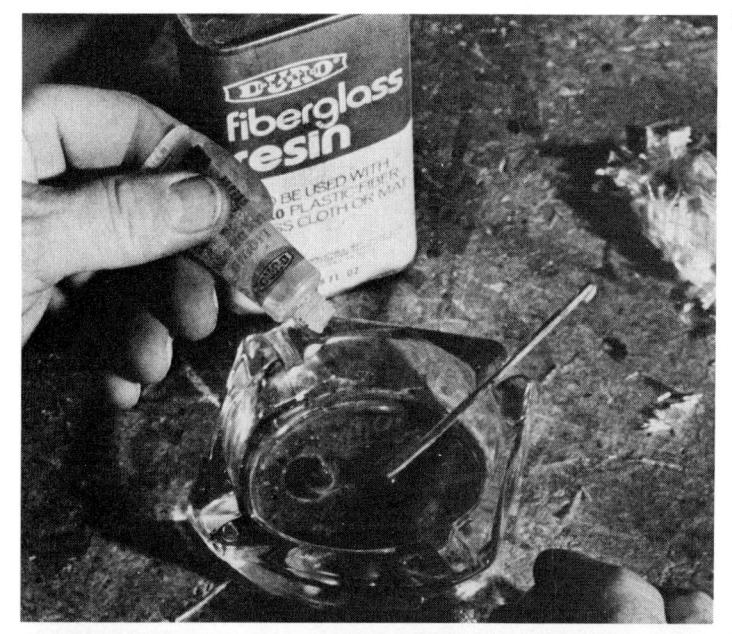

B. Resin is poured into small container, and hardener is added.

C. Chopped fiberglass is mixed into the resin with hardener added.

resin (to which you've added hardener), and stuff the mixture into the hole in the handle block or stick. Fill the hole completely before inserting the tang, then work the tang back and forth a few times to completely eliminate any air pockets.

Especially with short tangs, this gives a strength that I don't think can be beaten.

D. Mixture is packed into blind hole in short-tang construction; method works equally well for round-tang construction.

E. Short tang, with "teeth" filed alternately along its length, is introduced into blind hole filled with fiberglass, and worked back and forth to eliminate any air pockets.

F. Handle is clamped into place and fiberglass resin is allowed to cure for prescribed length of time.

CHAPTER 13

USING PINS AND CUTLER'S RIVETS

I don't suppose that cavemen used pins and rivets on their knives made of flint, but certainly they've been around just about as long as man has been making knives of steel. Modern epoxys have obviated the absolute *need* for these handy joining devices, but their use is still traditional and widespread. They are also darned attractive, as they carry the look of gleaming metal into full-tang handles that are otherwise devoid of relief.

Pins predate cutler's rivets by a few hundred years, so let's talk about them first. The most important thing to remember in selecting material from which to make pins is that it be resistant to corrosion. I've heard that some do-it-yourselfers use clipped nails, but I can't imagine a worse choice. For one thing, they aren't malleable enough to swell when peened and for another they rust.

I've used brazing rods, both brass and aluminum, for some time, but I believe my favorite choice on a couple of counts is plain old 10- or 12-gauge copper wire. All you have to do is strip the insulation, cut it to length, sharpen the point, and you're in business. Copper wire has the advantage of being totally rust proof, extremely malleable, and available anywhere. Moreover, a few feet of it will last you indefinitely if you don't go berserk and start rewiring the house.

Pins are used, nearly always, with full tangs, which means that holes drilled to receive them must pass through both tang and handle material. The procedure I follow is to drill holes where I want them in the tang, epoxy one scale to the tang, then using the tang holes as a guide, drill through the scale. I then epoxy the second scale into place, and drill through from the far side, using the holes already in place as a guide.

Some makers advise drilling pin holes after both scales are epoxied in place. This probably works okay if you're using a drill press, but when you go this route with a hand drill, you tend to enlarge the holes in the handle material in the process of drilling through the tang. My method takes longer (you've got to wait for the epoxy to cure twice), but it's foolproof.

Pins are one of the oldest methods of securing slabs to the tang in full-tang construction. Follow these steps for a perfect job:
A. With one scale rough shaped and epoxied to tang, drill pin holes through scale using tang holes as your guide.

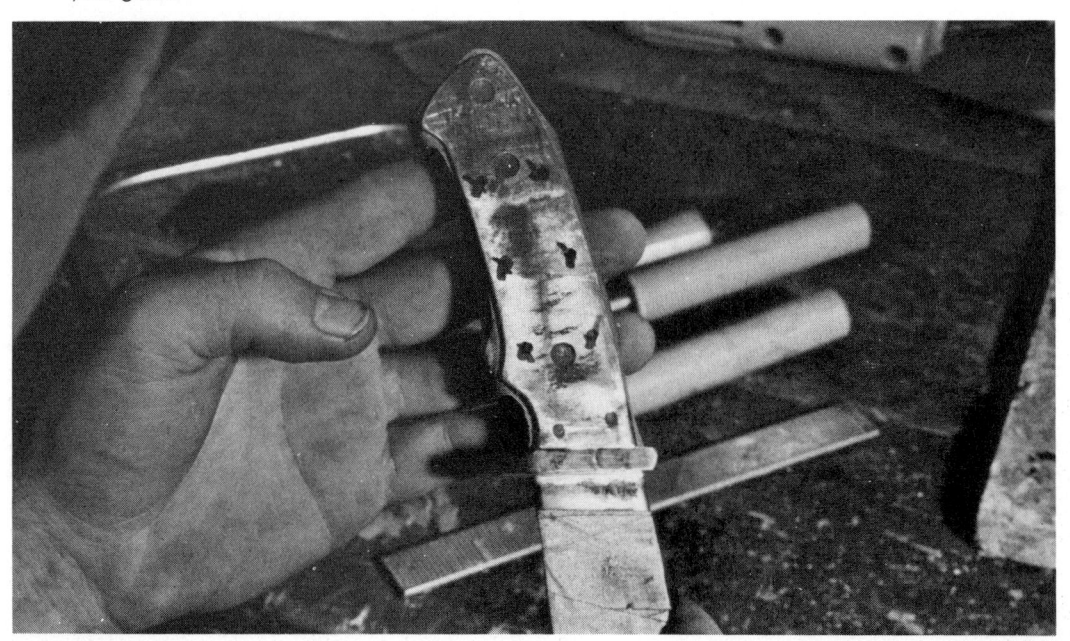

To set pins in handle material, you'll need two setting punches or nails ground to blunt tips. Punches or nails should be just a shade larger in diameter than the pins you are setting.

One punch is secured upright in a machinist's vise, and the other hit gently with a small (12-oz)

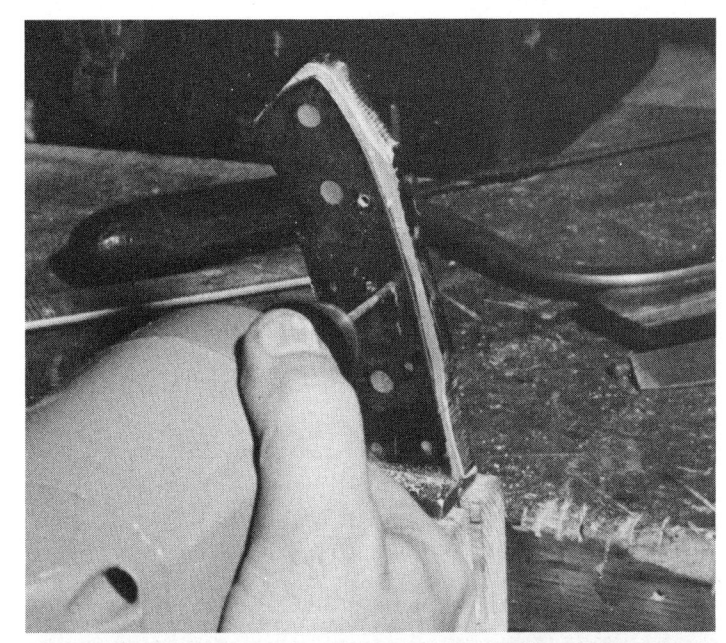

B. Pin holes are drilled through the scale with knife held in vice. Second scale will then be epoxied and drilled.

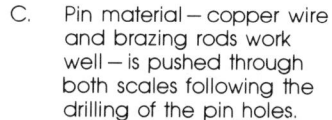

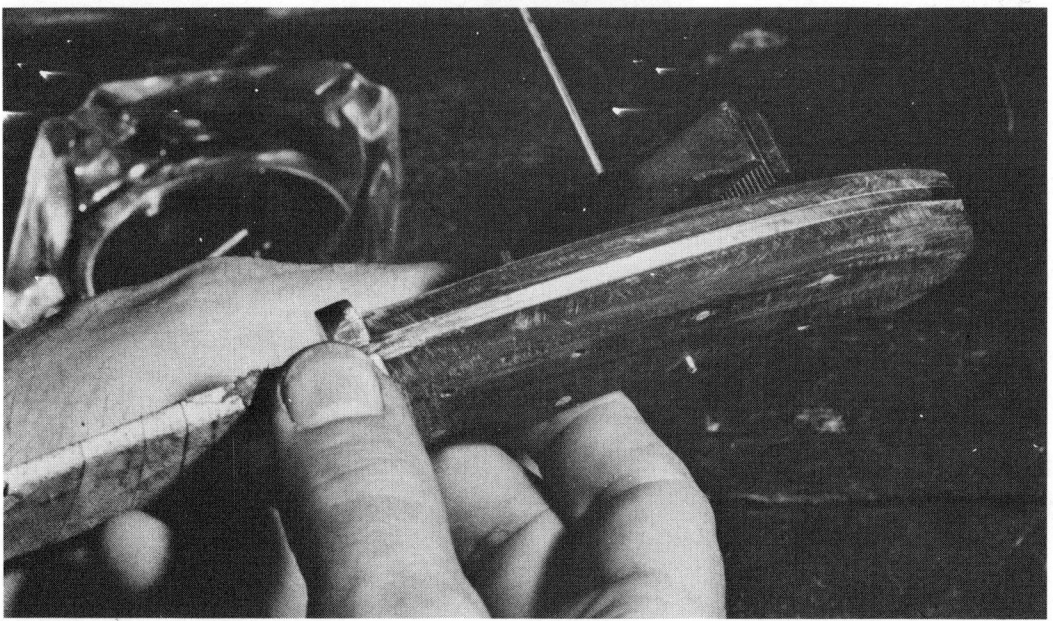

C. Pin material — copper wire and brazing rods work well — is pushed through both scales following the drilling of the pin holes.

D. Pins, after being cut to correct length, are ground to obtain flat ends.
E. This is what the pin will look like after being cut and ground to size.

ball peen hammer. Some makers like to countersink their handles slightly, and use tiny brass washers. I've never found a ready source for these washers, and don't really think they're required either.

Keep in mind, as you set your pins, that one false blow can mar your handle material if it's wood, or crack it if it's a relatively delicate material like stag. After the pins are set, grind and sand them flush with the handle. And, if you really want to go whole hog, coat your pins with clear epoxy before you drive them. They'll be with you for the lifetime of your knife.

HOW TO USE RIVETS

There are two ways to use cutler's rivets: The hard way and the easy way. I haven't found the easy way yet, so I'll tell you how I usually manage to muddle through the hard way.

To begin, three different sizes of holes are required for a really first-rate job. The smallest of these goes through the tang of the knife, and

F. Pins are set using punch; when handle material is wood and prone to split, two punches, as described in text, are preferable.

G. Final peening is done with light hammer to bring ends of pins nearly flush with surface of scales. Final flushing will be done on grinding and sanding wheels as scales are finished.

should be exactly the same diameter as the female portion of the rivet. The next largest of these holes goes through each scale, and should be fractionally larger than the female portion of the rivet. The largest hole, which is inlet into the surface of each scale, should be the same diameter as the head of

Steps to follow in using cutler's rivets:

A. With one scale epoxied to the tang, drill hole through scale using tang-hole as guide. Scale hole must then be enlarged from other side, as described in text.

B. With second scale now epoxied to tang, use previously drilled holes as guide to drill through second scale; again, enlarge scale holes to diameter slightly larger than that of the female portion of the rivet. This is essential to prevent scale from cracking when rivet is set.

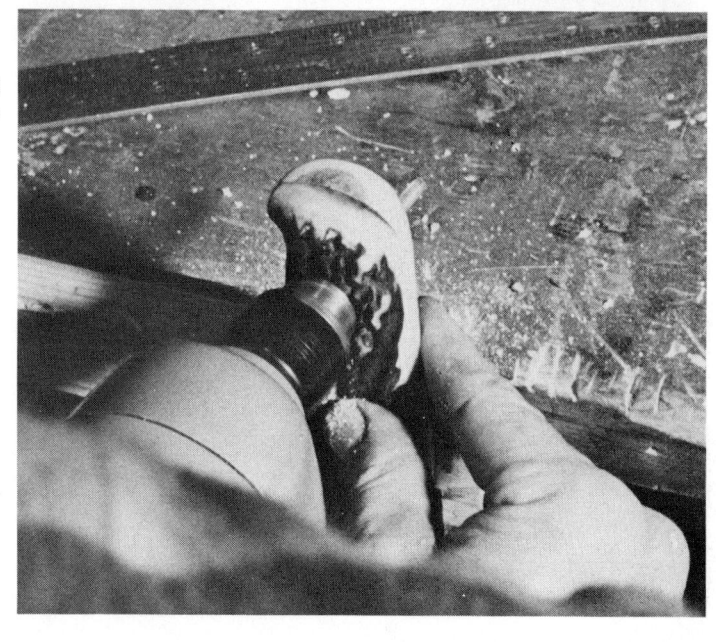

the rivet, and just the barest fraction of an inch deeper than the head is thick.

Not all rivets are exactly the same dimension, so I'm a little hesitant to give you bit dimensions. The rivets I'm using right now come from E. Christopher Firearms Company, and for them I

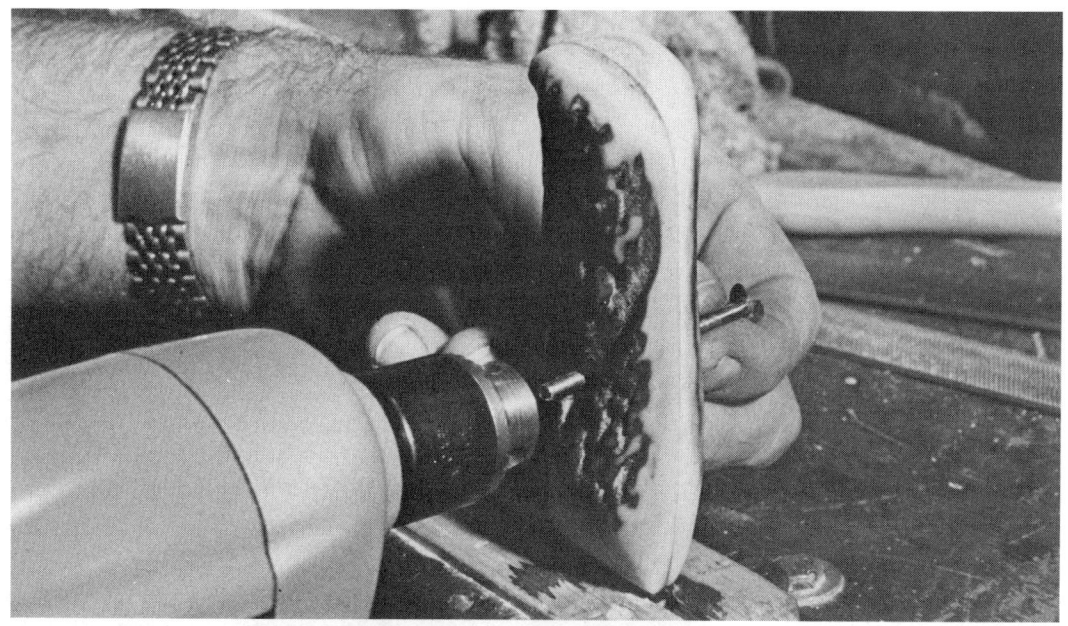

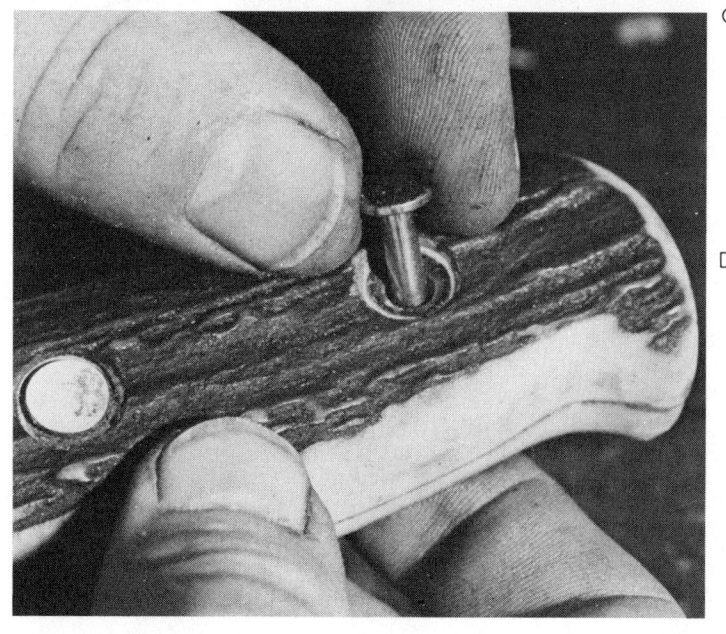

C. Using counter-boring tool described in text, drill holes in scales for rivet heads by chucking shaft of tool in drill and pulling drill toward you. Using this procedure, countersunk holes will be aligned perfectly.

D. Fit rivets into holes, and;

Cutler's Rivet

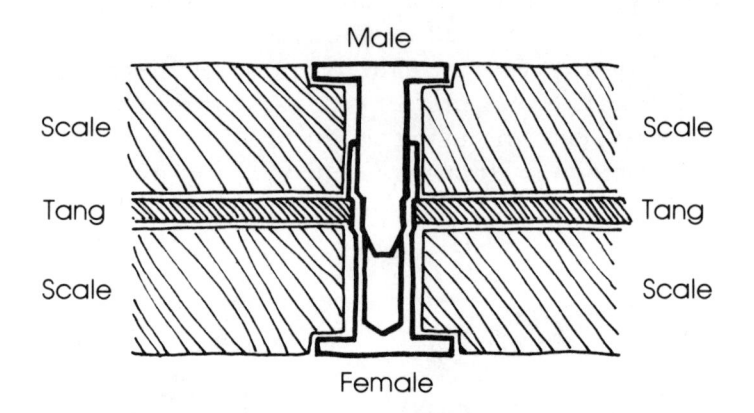

Scale — Male — Scale
Tang — Tang
Scale — Female — Scale

E. Set rivets by using two nails, the heads of which have been ground to the same size as the rivet heads. Use several light taps with hammer rather than hard strokes which may cause scales to crack.

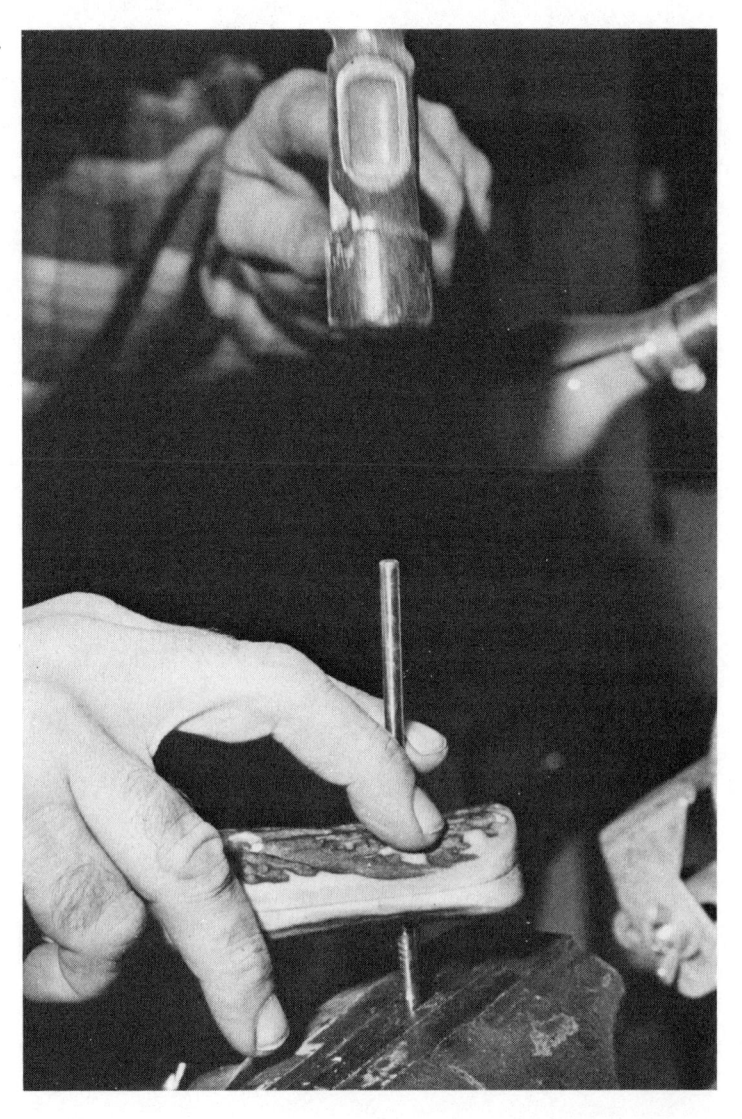

use a 5/32-inch bit for drilling the tang and a 3/16-inch bit for drilling the holes through the scales. Check your own; I make no guarantees.

I had a hard time getting the counter-sunk holes for the rivet heads exactly on center until I read the instruction sheet sent out by Indian Ridge Traders. Those knowledgeable folks advise using a common nail with a head the same size as that of the rivet head. You put the blade in a vise, push the nail through the holes in the scales and tang, and chuck the nail in your drill on the other side. To countersink, you pull the drill toward you, and the little ridges on the underside of the nail head drill your countersink hold precisely on center. Clever, huh?

I found that using an unaltered nail worked fine on the softer woods such as maple, but on harder woods and stag, it tended to burn rather badly. To overcome this, I started with a slightly larger nail, and fashioned the counter-boring tool you see pictured here. You can make one in about 10 minutes with nothing more than a file, punch, and grinder. I polished mine so it would photograph nicely, but that doesn't make it cut a bit

Counter-boring tool described in text is used for drilling perfectly aligned holes for cutler's rivets. Photo at left shows author sharpening the tool with a needle file, and at right is a close-up of the tool, made from grinding and polishing a nail.

better. Just remember that it's the *lower* lip that does the cutting as you pull the drill toward you. So everything is backward from the way you'd normally make a cutting tool.

I think you'll probably be able to understand the procedure for drilling the three different sizes of rivet holes better by referring to the accompanying photographs than by my belaboring the point further in the text. I'll mention one more fairly obvious point, and let it alone: Because the tang hole is smaller than the scale holes, you must drill both initially in the smaller 5/32-inch size, then drill from the outside in, to enlarge it to 3/16-inch. Follow the illustrations and I don't think you'll have any problem.

Rivets are set in pretty much the same manner as pins, except here you're better off using nails with heads the same size as that of the rivet. Mount one in your vise and strike the other with your ball peen hammer. (The knife handle and rivet, meanwhile, are hopefully somewhere in between.)

Again, proceed slowly!

CHAPTER 14

FINISHING YOUR KNIFE: Sanding, Buffing, and Polishing

The final look of your knife depends a lot on the time and care you devote to sanding, buffing, and polishing it. A poorly finished knife may cut almost (but not quite) as good as one that's well done, but it'll never be something you want to show to your friends.

Hilts, handles, and pommels require sanding as part of the shaping process. A sanding disc will remove soft metal almost as fast as it will hardwood, so the point at which you transfer your hilt and pommel from the grinding wheel to the sanding disc is pretty much up to you. I do nearly all my handle shaping on a sanding disc, then sand it smooth with an orbital sander or by hand.

You may also want to do some sanding on your blade, whether you have ground your own or customized a finished one. This will remove the grinder marks, but still leave sanding scratches. A better way is to go from the grinder to medium grit buffing compound, and finally to red rouge.

The best sandpaper I've found for hand sanding or use on an orbital sander is a waterproof silicon carbide product made by the 3-M Company. It's called *Wetordry Tri-M-Ite,* and it can be purchased by name at many hardware stores. Use it in progressively smaller grits down to 400 before going to a buffing wheel dressed with red rouge. If you sand your blade, wet sanding along its length will produce superior results.

For disc-sanding using your bench-mounted drill, it's best to forget about regular sandpaper and go to discs cut from emery cloth. Better yet are the heavy duty grinding discs such as used for automobile refinishing and the like. The finest grade is an 80-grit, and that's as coarse as you want to use for knife-making.

Although the heavy duty discs are bonded to thin fiberboard, they seem to work better when backed by a 6-inch rubber pad. These discs are fairly expensive (about $2.50), but they have two usable sides and last quite a while.

A relatively new product that I like a lot is made by brazing tungsten carbide grit to a thin sheet of steel. These are available in either 4-inch or 6-inch sizes, and are intended for use on a rubber pad of comparable dimension. Sears stores stock both sizes, with the 4-inch number going for about $1.60. I don't know how long these things last, because I've only been using mine about four months, and it still looks like new.

BUFFING AND POLISHING WHEELS

Frequent mention already has been made of buffing compounds, so now let's talk a little about the wheels where the compound is used.

A point worth making more than once is that you must have separate wheels for each grade of compound you use. Three wheels will see you through: One for medium (320) grit compound, a second for fine (600) grit compound, and a third for red rouge. If you want to get a fourth, dress it with white rouge for polishing your handles.

Buffing wheels are regularly sold in 6-, 8-, and 10-inch diameters. The 6-inch size works nicely on a bench-mounted drill or bench grinder. The wheels themselves are simply multiple layers of muslin stitched together. They also make a loose muslin wheel for cleanup between different grit sizes, and for final polishing.

Steps to follow in setting up a buffing wheel:

A. Using contact (latex-base) cement, bond two or three thicknesses of stitched-muslin buffing wheels together; the broader the working surface, the easier and faster the buffing job will be.

B. When cement has "glazed," line up discs and press together tightly. Allow to cure 20 minutes.

Most stitched-muslin wheels in the 6-inch size come in thicknesses of about ⅜-inch. This means you have to glue two or three together to get a good working surface. Alternatively, you can glue a single thickness to a rubber pad. Two wheels glued together are about right for use with a drill; but for use on a bench grinder you should use three, or as many as necessary to fill the grinder's arbor. Three discs, glued together, give a working surface of about 1¼ inches.

I see little value to having mirror finishes on the blades of working knives, but if you want one on your wall hanger, you'll need to get a felt polishing wheel and dress it with white rouge. Felt wheels comes in three different finishes (soft, medium, and hard), with the hard giving the highest polish. Felt is expensive, running about $10 in the 6-inch diameter. These wheels are usually an inch wide, so only one is needed.

Sears carries muslin buffing wheels, but you'll likely have to go further afield for felt polishing wheels.

I know that Brownells stocks them, and Herter's may have them also. Stoeger carried them at one time, but I believe they've dropped them from their line.

D. Put buffing wheel on bench grinder and true it with a stone as described in text.

E. If using Cherry Corners' compound, paint liberally on the surface of the wheel and allow to dry per manufacturer's instructions.

F. Use felt-tip marker to mark grit on the dressed wheel; each grit requires its own wheel.

G. After compound has cured for a day, break it up by striking the wheel against a hard surface.

H. Use a piece of scrap metal to smooth the wheel prior to use. Single application will see you through several knives.

"TRUING" MUSLIN BUFFING WHEELS

There's a simple trick for getting good results from buffing wheels. It's called "truing," and it is about as messy a job as you'll get into in your knifemaking activities.

After you've glued your wheels together using a rubber-base cement such as Pliobond, mount them on your drill or bench grinder. With the motor on, hold a truing stone or brick against the wheel. This gets rid of all the excess "fluff" and establishes a good flat working surface. Sears sells an all-purpose silicon sharpening stone that works okay for this purpose or you can buy a regular truing brick. In a pinch an ordinary piece of concrete building block will get the job done. You'll likely need to use your truing stone periodically thereafter as the wheel wears and new compound is added.

Truing your wheel the first time sends a shower of muslin flying all over the place, and you'll look like you've been on the losing end of a pillow fight when you get done. Still, it's a necessary job and one you don't want to overlook.

MORE ABOUT BUFFING COMPOUNDS

I know I've already mentioned buffing and polishing compounds several times, but since they are an unfamiliar subject to most home hobbyists, I want to touch on them one final time.

A number of different compounds are available through conventional outlets. Sears, for example, sells a four-stick box of the stuff, for about $2. This includes a black emery cake for rough work, a brown rouge for soft metals, red rouge for steel, and white rouge for putting high polishes on steel. White rouge is also what you want to use for final buffing on your handle.

Brownells stocks a line of compounds it calls Polish-O-Ray in four grits down to 500, plus a polishing compound in 555-grit.

The buffing compounds made by Cherry Corners Mfg. Co. of Lodi, Ohio, are unusual enough to warrant further comment. Cherry Corners is the offshoot of a gun shop of the same name, well-known throughout the Midwest for its fine gunsmiths.

The proprietors developed their compound after growing weary of constantly having to redress their buffing wheels with conventional stick compound that wouldn't stay on long enough to get through a normal barrel-buffing operation.

Their compound comes in five grits, from 80 to 600, and is applied as a liquid that is then allowed to dry for 24 hours before use. You then break it up by giving it a few good whacks on some hard surface, smooth the wheel with a piece of scrap metal (I use a railroad spike), and then have at it. A single application will get you through several blades, and it's easy to reapply.

The stuff sells for around $3 per half-pound jar, and a half a jar will dress a 6-inch wheel. I recommend it highly.

POLISHING HANDLES

Any reasonably hard surface will polish. This includes hardwoods, leather, stag, Micarta, horn, and

As described in the text, almost any hard surface will buff to a nice finish. The author uses several different grades of stick compound for steel, soft metals, and handle materials. Here he is shown, below, applying white rouge to a muslin wheel, and then (right) using the dressed wheel to polish a stag handle. Red and brown rouge are other common grades.

other commonly used knife-handle materials. How high a luster it takes depends a lot on its porosity; hence the denser exotic woods take a higher gloss than do their American counterparts.

After you finish sanding your handle (regardless of its composition) with 400-grit paper, put it on a buffing wheel dressed with medium to fine grit compound. Brown or red rouge work equally well.

Unless you do an exceptionally good job of sanding, scratches that you didn't see before will show up when you begin buffing. Alternate between buffing and sanding until the last of these scratches disappears. At the same time you are sanding and buffing your handle material, do the same thing with your hilt and pommel. If the alignment between handle and pommel, and handle and hilt isn't perfect, now is the time to correct it. Take your time and do it right.

From time to time as you progress, wipe the knife clean with chlorinated hydrocarbon (carbochlor) or a similar cleaning solvent. Lava soap and water, used in combination with a soft brush, also work well.

Another good trick, especially for wood, is to use linseed or mineral oil with medium (FF) grade pumice stone powder. Dip a clean rag in oil, then in the powder, and then rub the handle like mad. It will give you a smoother finish than anything I know.

Now for final polishing, change to a muslin wheel dressed with white rouge. Keep at it until you've brought the handle and soft metal to as high a luster as it will take. Twenty minutes on the white-rouge wheel is usually about what it takes.

Finally, wipe off any buffing compound that adheres to your work and put a sheep's wool or loose muslin wheel on your drill. Hold your handle to this for a few minutes to obtain the deepest possible gloss finish.

The exotic hardwoods and most of the synthetics require no final treatment, but leather, the domestic hardwoods, and some stag will benefit from oil or wax. Minwax makes an antique oil finish that is good for use on wood or stag, and the gunstock finishes—such as those made by Birchwood Casey, Lin-Speed, and Tru-Oil—are without peer.

Tandy Leather Company is probably your best bet for finishes that preserve and protect leather. A product they call Neat-Lac does wonders for leather handles, and even sheaths to boot. And plain old Johnson's paste wax works fine on just about anything.

Nearly all of the oil and wax treatments should be followed by a final polishing with sheep's wool or loose muslin for best results. Man can do no more.

CHAPTER 15

THE SHEATH: How to Design and Make It

The sheath has provided a home for the working knife since some early-day backwoodsman told his buddy his finger was about to fall off. If you're going to do anything with your knife except hang it on the wall, you've got to have a sheath to put it in. Why else would cows grow leather?

Good leather is the key to good sheathmaking. And although prices have soared in recent years, it's still possible to buy in almost any town enough scrap leather to build a sheath for every knife.

I began sheath-making several years before I did knife-making, simply because I figured I could do a better job than the machine at the factory. Sheaths for store-bought knives have improved a lot in the past few years, but I'm still partial to the homegrown variety.

WHAT KIND OF LEATHER?

Latigo is the best leather there is for sheath-making—period. It works easily, wet-forms well, and takes dye like a dream. It's also, unfortunately, one of the most expensive leathers you can buy.

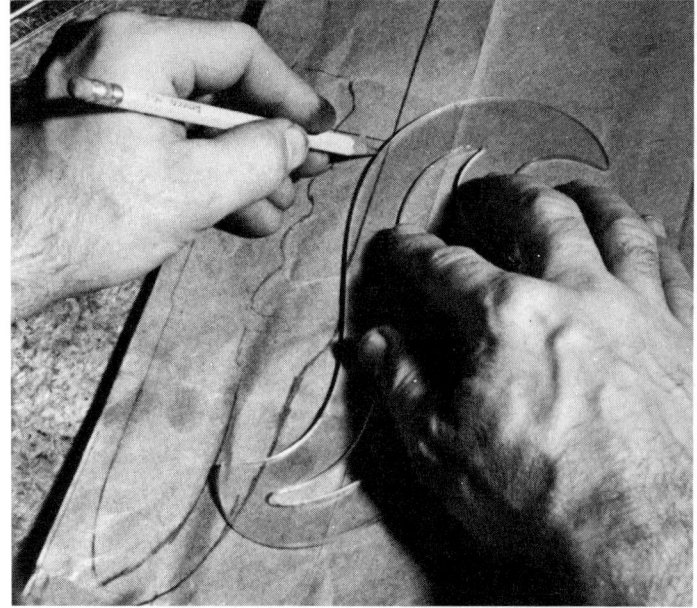

Steps to follow in building a sheath:
A. With outline of knife traced on heavy brown paper, author uses straight edge to mark outline of sheath; paper is folded so that pattern will be repeated when cut.

B. Author used french curve to mark convex and concave portions of the design.

If the price of latigo staggers you, any good harness leather will do. I make my sheaths to carry my knives not just to tool them, so the heavily oiled harness leathers are no problem to me. If you view the situation similarly, this may be the route you will want to take.

Leathers come in about as many weights or

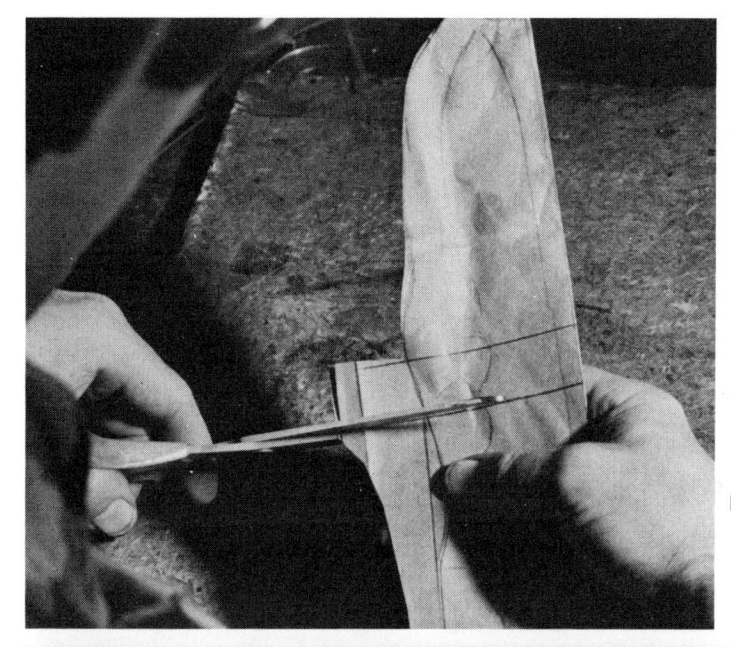

C. With paper still folded, design is cut out.

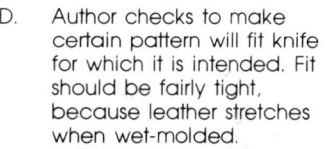

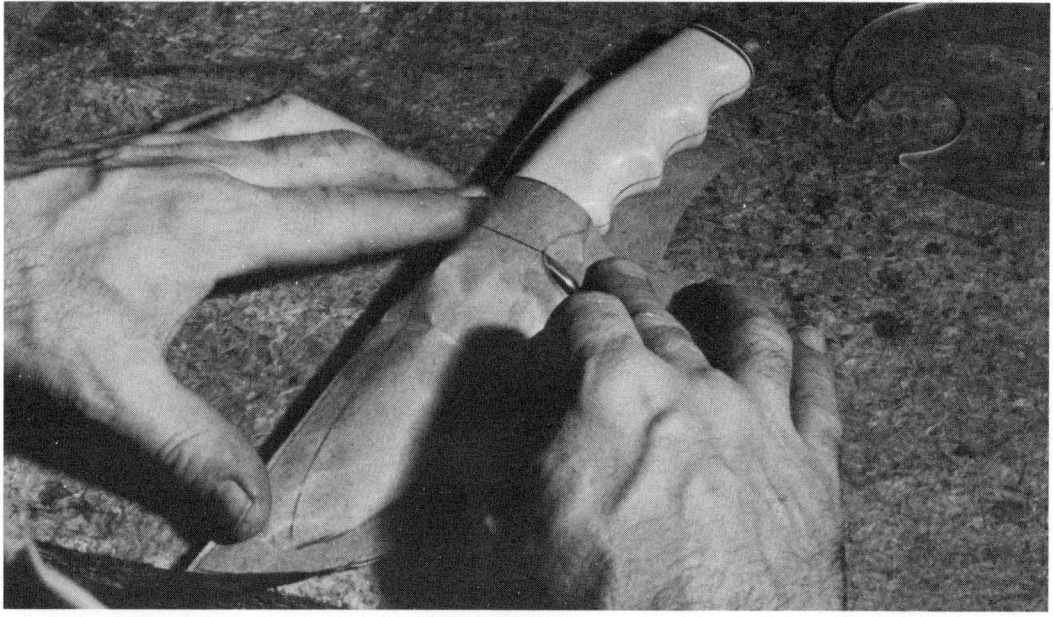

D. Author checks to make certain pattern will fit knife for which it is intended. Fit should be fairly tight, because leather stretches when wet-molded.

thicknesses as they do varieties. While it's obvious that you won't have to house your bird knife in as heavy a sheath as you do your Bowie, you do want a fair amount of cowhide between you and the cutting edge of your belt pal while you're busting through brush. For most purposes, 8-to-10 ounce leather serves well. The thickness of 8-oz leather

E. Pattern is traced onto rough side of the leather. Care should be taken at this point to make sheath left- or right-handed, as desired.

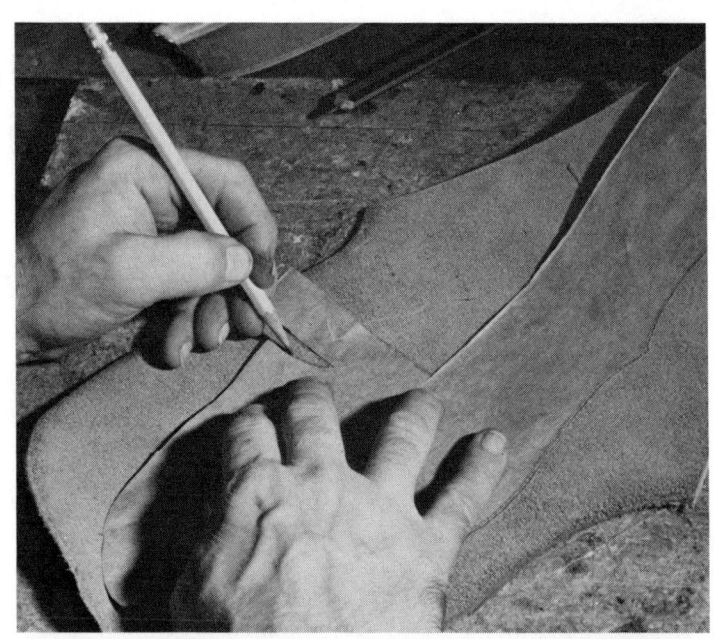

F. Author views the completed tracing. Concave cutout on right side at top will be made after pattern is cut and folded, to achieve precise cut.

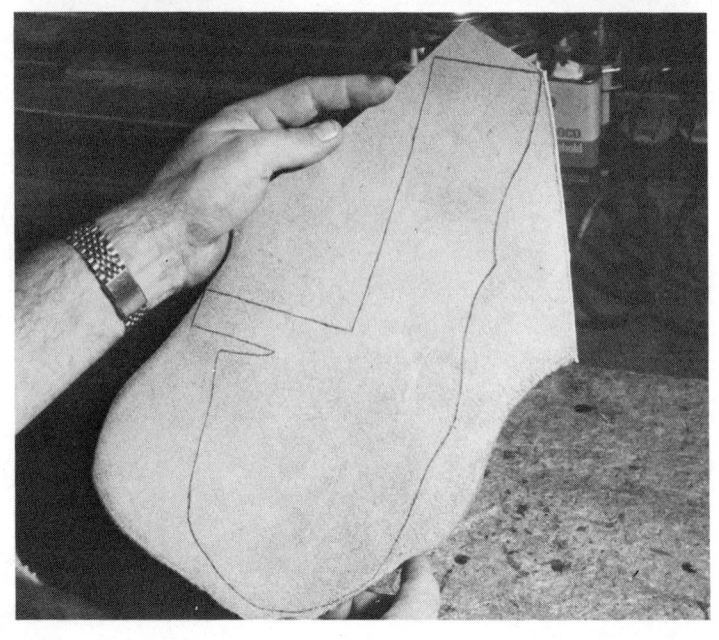

G. Using patch knife or utility knife, leather is cut. For straight edges, cut should only be made once, so sharp blade is essential.

is 8/64-inch or ⅛-inch and the thickness of 10-oz leather is 10/64 inch. (I know those aren't the lowest common denominators, but that's the way leather is measured.)

If you live so far out in the sticks that you can't find a local source for leather, write to: Tandy, 2808 Shamrock, Fort Worth TX 76107. Have them send you their current catalog too. Tandy isn't the cheapest source by a long shot but anything you get from them will be good quality.

TOOLS YOU WILL NEED

The tools you'll need for sheath-making aren't that many or that expensive. You need a couple of big needles for saddle stitching, a punch if you plan to lace your sheath or use rivets, and a good sharp knife. It's handy to have a thronging chisel with at least three prongs, but you can make a one-prong chisel that serves the purpose by simply grinding down a nail. It's probably also possible to grind your own rivet setter, but for the mere $1.50 these things cost, it's hardly worth the trouble.

156

H. With creases made in pattern, author begins gluing. For necessary flexibility, only a rubber-base cement should be used.

Some Typical Sheath Designs

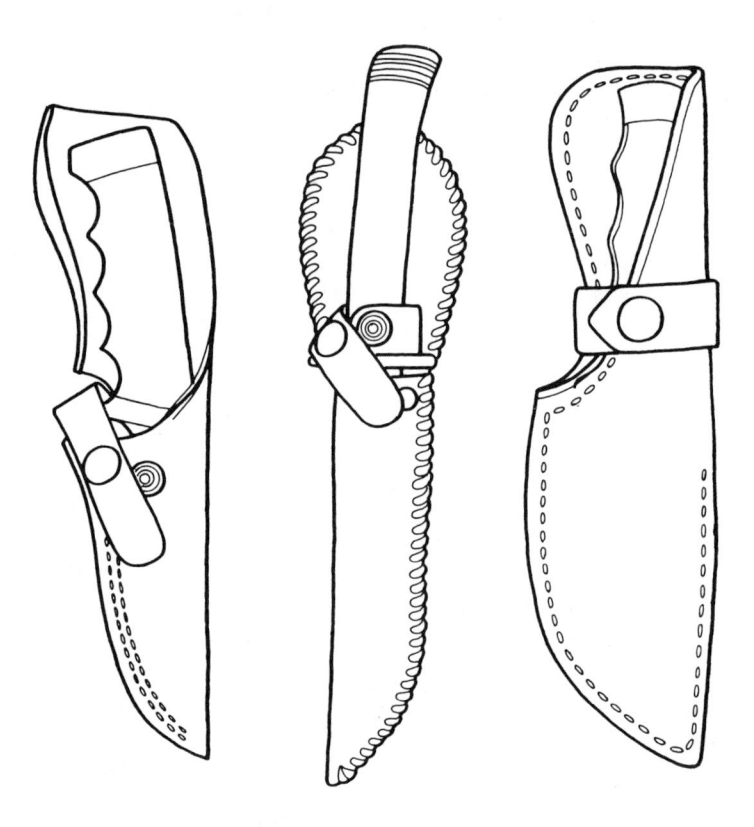

Anything you need or can think of is available from Tandy, and most hobby shops carry a modest selection of leather-working tools also.

If you're thinking about buying an awl, my advice is save your money. Two needles will get the job done faster and better. I can't think of anything else you really need to have.

DESIGNING YOUR SHEATH

The list of innovative sheath designs is almost endless, but there are really only two basic types: wrap-around and double-edge. The double-edge can be cut from smaller pieces of leather but it takes twice as much stitching or lacing and due to

Some Typical Sheath Designs

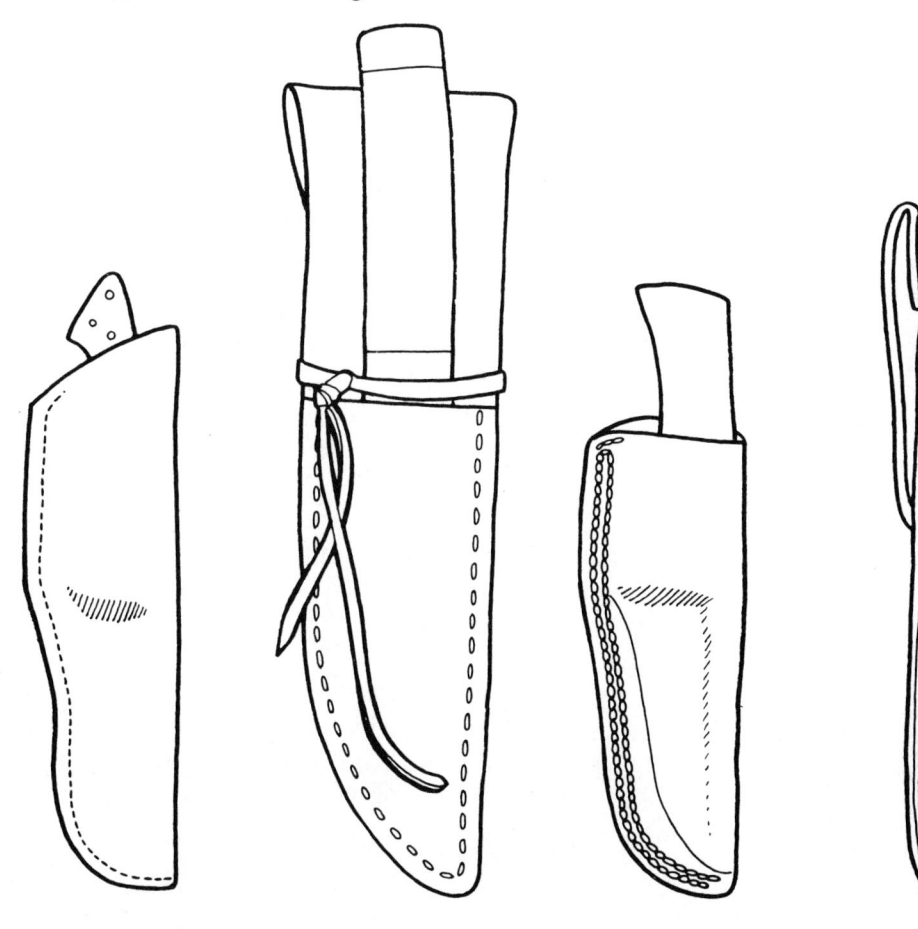

1. Using special knife, author skives the welt. Patch knife works well here, too, if skiving knife is not available.

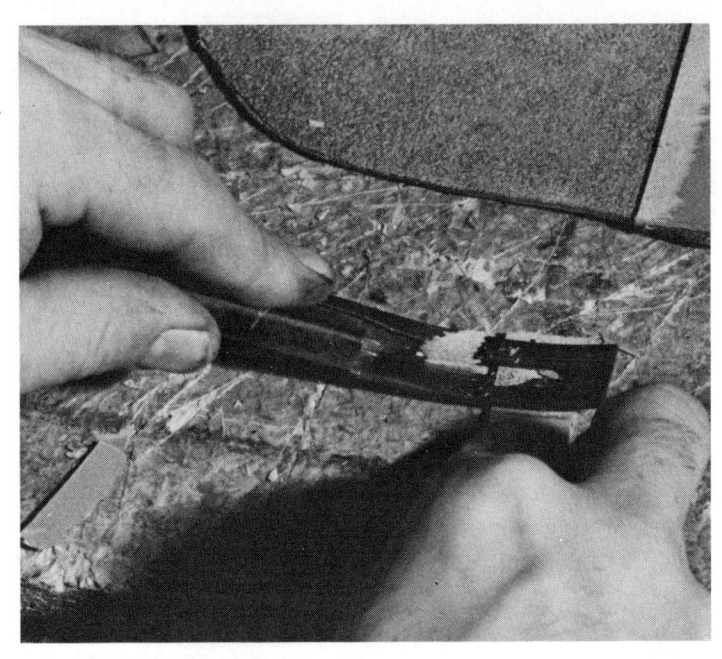

my inherently lazy nature, I seldom fool with them. Besides, I like the looks of the wrap-around style beter.

I'm now going to be painfully honest with you. When I want to try a new design I thumb through my outdoor magazines and catalogs to see what new designs the quality knife manufacturers have come up with lately. My attitude is, why tax my brain when I can have some fancy design artist work for me for free? I can't think of a better design than the pouch-style used by Buck, if the hilt of your knife is small. It has a button-down flap that makes it just about impossible to lose your knife. The molded-pouch design used by Gerber is another one of my favorites.

I've developed my own semi-pouch design that I like better than anything else I've seen. It's what I've used in the illustrations to show you the step-by-step construction. Its advantage to me is its one-piece construction, which has got to mean greater strength and longer wear. The same basic construction techniques are used with almost any design you select.

159

J. With welt glued in place, both edges of the sheath are cemented.

K. Sheath is held in vise for 15 minutes to allow cement to cure.

L. Spur-spacer is used to make pattern for slits.

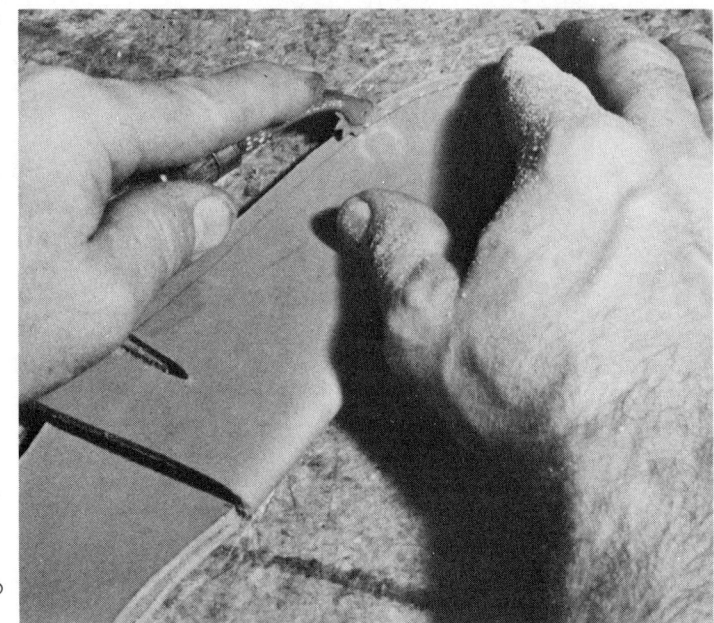

M. Eight-prong thonging tool is used to cut slits for saddle-stitching. Three-prong tool, in background, will be used to go around curved area.

Using rivets is something else you'll have to decide on yourself. Most knife-makers supply sheaths that aren't riveted, but their sheaths are usually double-stitched by machine. I do my stitching by hand, use only single stitching, and usually pop in a couple of rivets at stress points. It all depends, I guess, on one's view of what constitutes aesthetics and how rugged the duty you expect your sheath to perform.

The main thing to keep in mind as you design your sheath is the basic purpose it will serve. For a fighting knife, you obviously want a sheath that will allow you to have your knife in your hand in a hurry. For a hunting or skinning blade, protection of you and the knife is the main consideration. If the sheath is functional and well built, it's a good design.

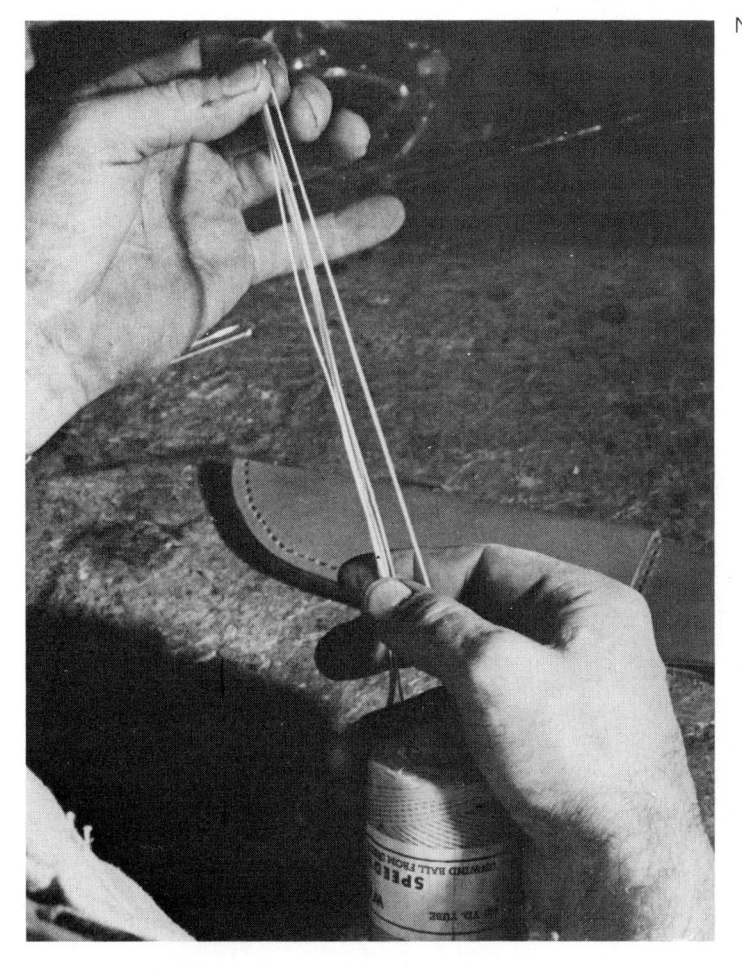

N. Author measures out waxed nylon thread to be used for stitching; length of thread should be approximately six times length of area to be stitched.

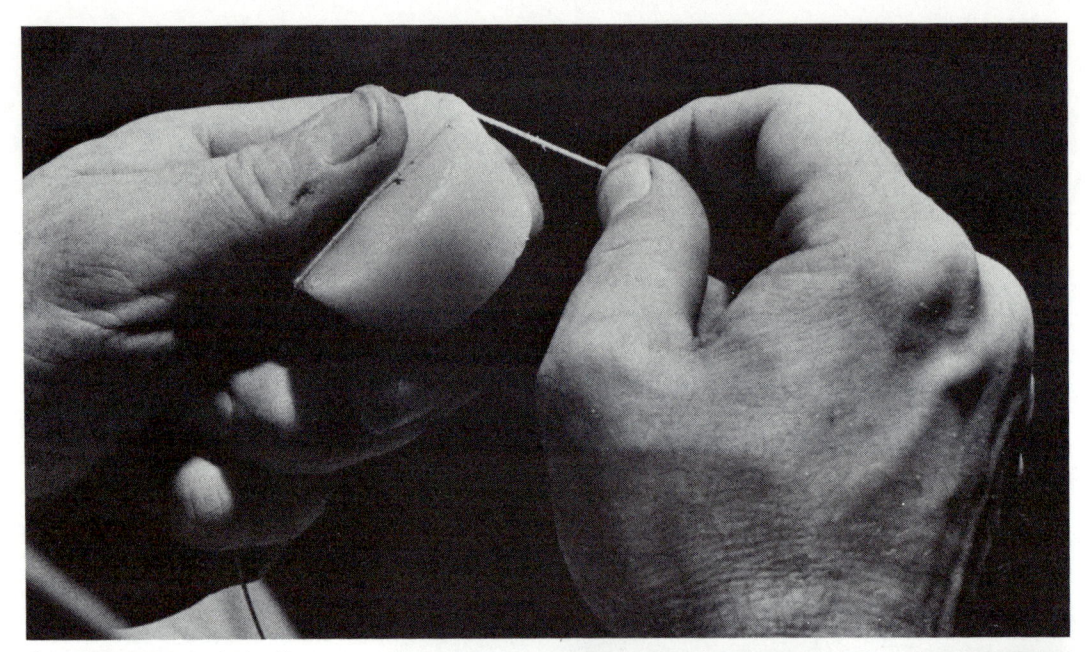

O. Thread is coated with beeswax to give it additional strength and wear-resistance.

P. Author begins saddle stitch in upper left-hand corner of the sheath. Note that both needles are being pushed through the same slit.

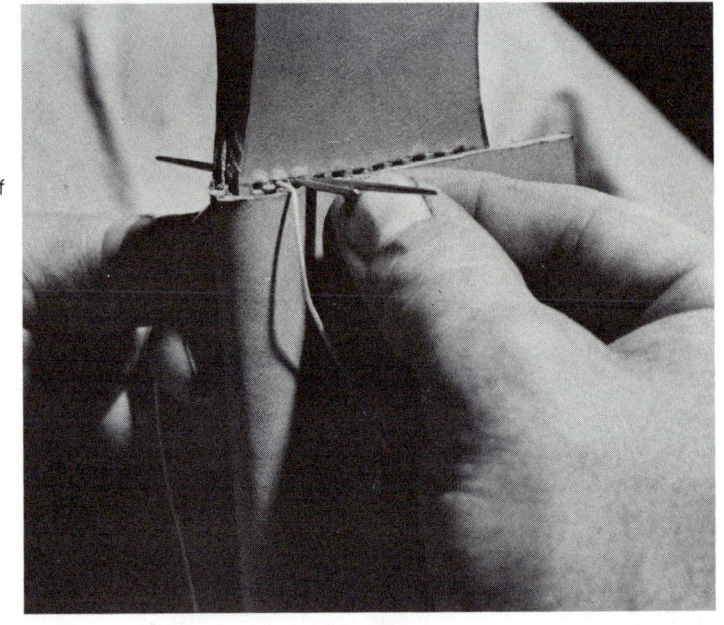

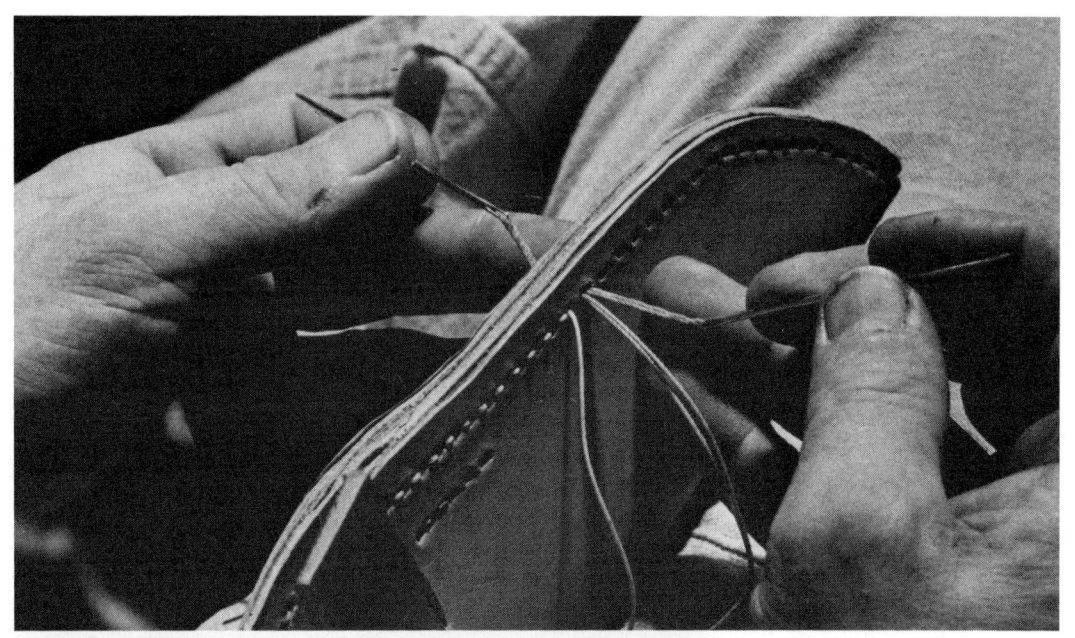

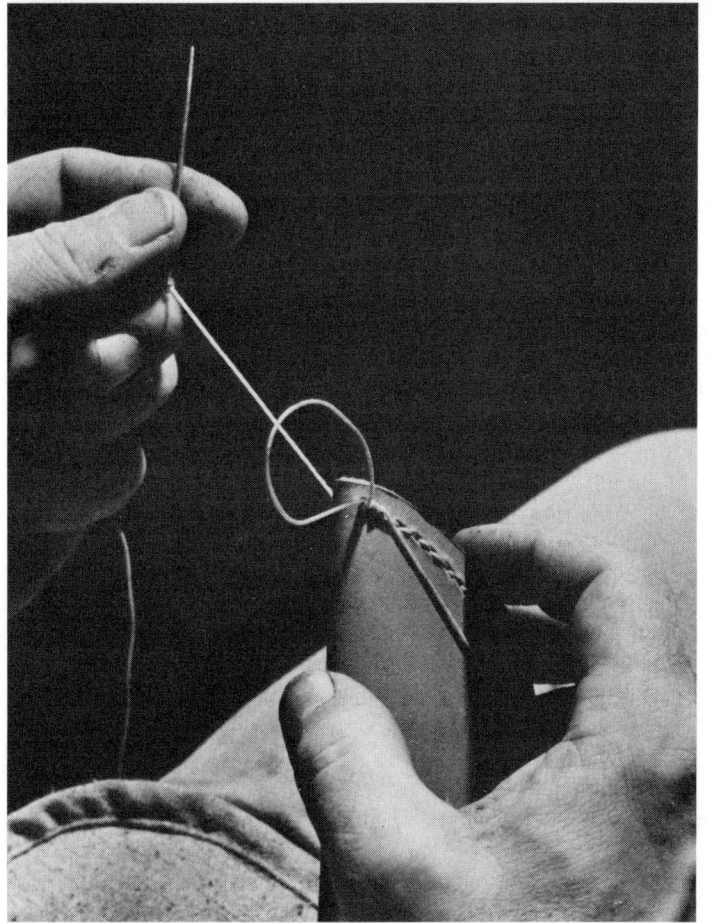

Q. Stitching is about three-fourths completed. The author likes to hold sheath in his lap throughout the stitching operation.

R. With stitching completed, thread is tied off on backside of sheath and stitched through again before cutting.

S. With stitching completed, sheath is immersed in water for about 20 minutes in preparation for wet forming.

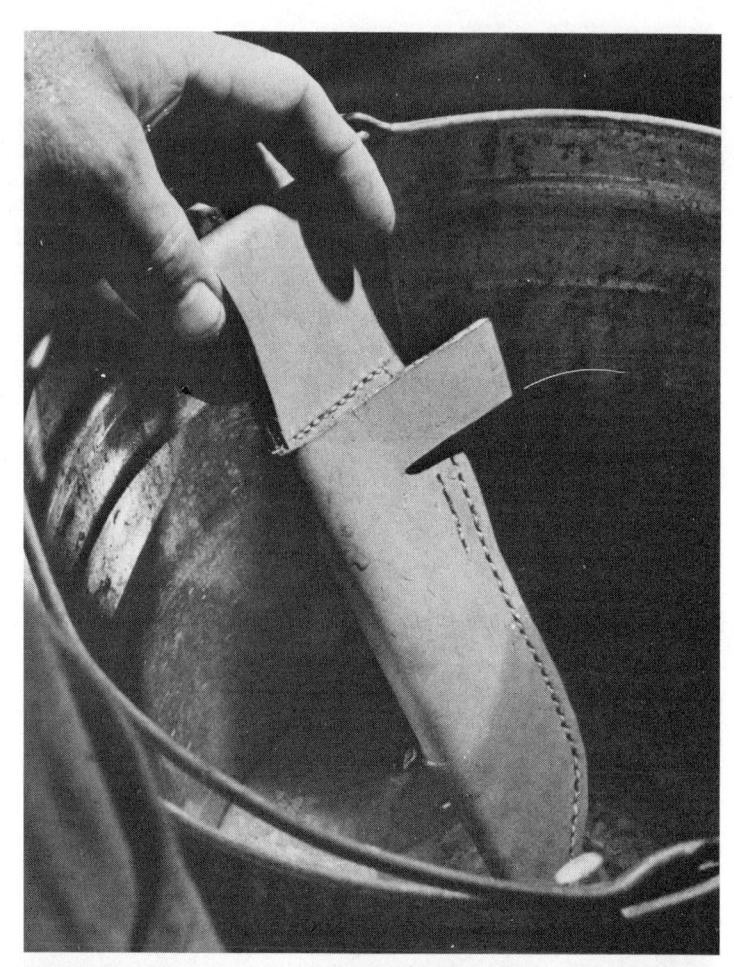

T. Knife is wrapped in polyethylene wrap to protect it during wet-forming; this is a habit the author picked up from wet-forming pistol holsters.

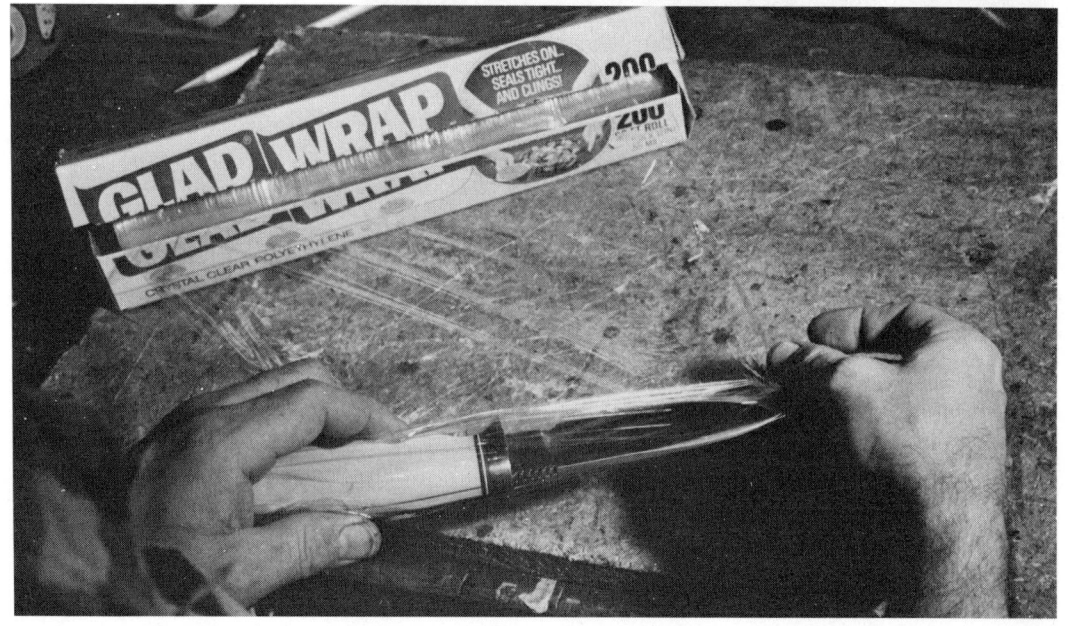

165

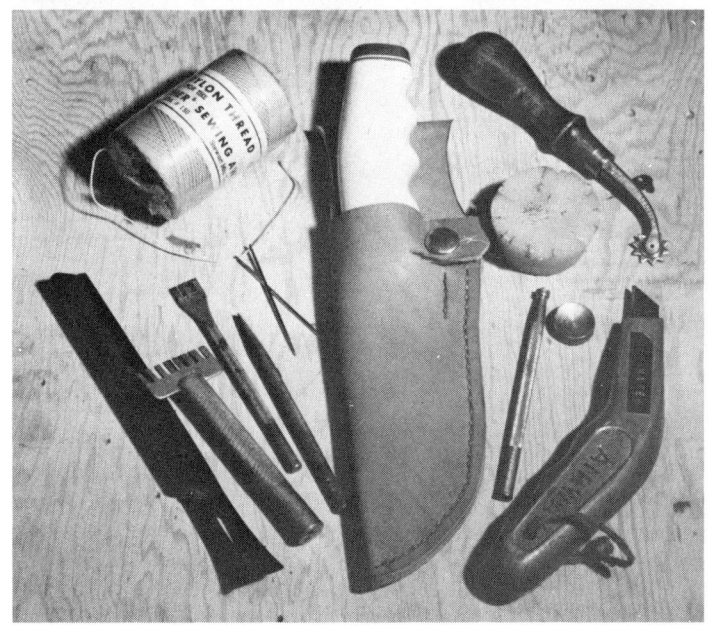

U. Wrapped knife is pushed into wet sheath and left overnight for leather to dry. When dry, leather will conform to the contours of the knife.

V. The completed sheath, with tools used in the operation.

CHAPTER 16

KNIFE CARE: Honing and Other Thoughts

Proper sharpening of a knife is no more difficult than the proper use of one. Some folks have tried to make honing sound difficult, though, and there must be a jillion different sharpeners on the market—every one of them guaranteed to give you the perfect edge.

I'm a great believer in free enterprise and anyone who can make and sell a gadget that will do *anything* right has my respect and admiration. But I'll tell you right now, and I'm even ready to argue with anyone who disagrees, absolutely nothing will sharpen your blade better than a soft Arkansas oilstone.

One small corner of Arkansas is blessed with a naturally occurring type of rock known as novaculite that is particularly well suited to make sharpening stones. There's a lot of novaculite around but the Arkansas variety seems to have fewer impurities and a better texture than most.

This stuff began its life millions of years ago as sandstone and then through just the right combination of geologic heat and pressure was transformed into the extremely hard, fine-grain material that is quarried today to make sharpening stones. Man has never been able to improve on good novaculite as a knife-sharpening tool and I doubt that he ever will.

Arkansas oilstones come in two different grades or types: the soft, off-white stone that's right for about 90 percent of your sharpening chores; and a hard, nearly black stone that's used for razors, surgical instruments, and—if you wish—putting a razor edge on your knife. I have both, but find I use the soft stone nearly all the time.

GETTING A GOOD OILSTONE

Nature doesn't always do a perfect job (even in Texas and Arkansas), and there's a fair amount of difference in the quality of Arkansas oilstones. Some have dark streaks caused by impurities. Others have naturally occurring pits or hairline cracks, or slight imperfections (chips and such) that occur in the finishing process.

Reputable suppliers sell these blemished stones as seconds, and charge about half price for them. Not-so-reputable suppliers have been known to try to palm off these imperfect stones at full price. Imperfect stones will still sharpen your blade, no mistake about that. They just won't do it quite as well.

There are two ways to be sure you get a perfect stone. One is to know what you're looking for, then go to a good sporting goods store that sells them and rummage through the lot until you find what you're after. Because I'm something of an impulse buyer, this is usually the route I take. The other, probably better way to get the best Arkansas oilstone money will buy, is to order it from the A. G. Russell Company. This outfit likely throws out more stones than a lot of suppliers sell, and any you get from them will be top quality.

Russell's current catalog lists an 8-inch soft bench stone at $18 and a hard surgical stone of the

Making a bench stand or block for your oilstone is a simple matter. Above, the author inlets a soft pine block with mallet and chisel, and at right he finishes the inlet well with a Moto-Tool. Total time invested: 39 minutes.

same size at $38. Pocket stones from Russell fetch about $4 to $7. Pocket stones are okay for touch-ups in the field but not much else.

SETTING UP YOUR BENCH STONE

There's only one way to do a first rate job of sharpening a sheath knife: Use *both* hands and a bench stone. Right off, you can see that if you're going to use both hands to sharpen your knife, you probably think that you've got to have the stone fixed to the bench. You're right, you do.

There are two ways I know to do this. One is to clamp your sharpening stone in your bench vise and the other is to use the stone with a stand that's clamped to the workbench or some equally sturdy surface. Using a vise tends to limit the places where you can use your stone, so it's better to use a stand. Russell sells a good one made of cast aluminum for about $8. It has indentations for "C" clamps and an oil reservoir.

Alternatively, at no cost except about an hour's worth of your time, you can make your own stand from a block of soft pine. Use small

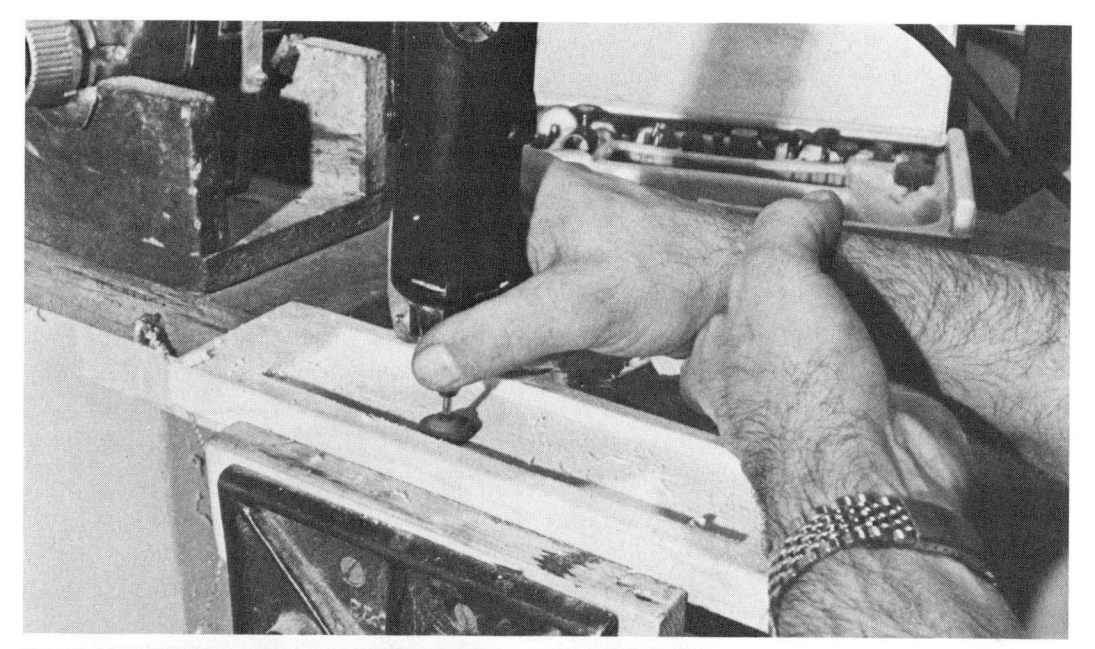

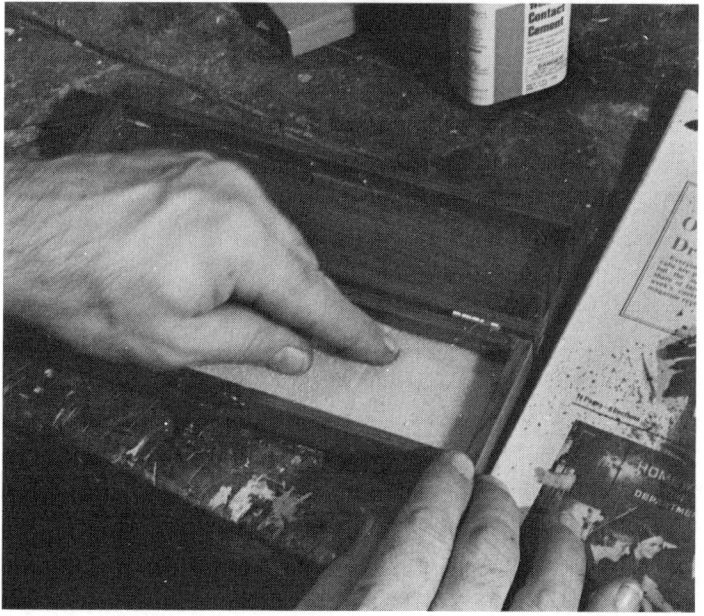

As described in the text, a thin piece of foam rubber glued inside the oilstone provides an oil reservoir that is particularly handy for field use.

pieces of quarter-round to hold the stone in place or inlet the pine board with a wood chisel. The latter version packs and stores a little easier, so I prefer it.

Make your bench stand plain or fancy; it doesn't matter. Just be sure to allow a couple of inches on each end for clamps. That's the only function the stand has to serve—a way to hold your stone on the bench.

A good many suppliers furnish little cedar boxes with the Arkansas oilstones. These are good, because they protect the stones from damage and also provide a handy means of keeping your stone bathed in oil. To accomplish the latter, cut and glue a thin piece of foam rubber to the inside top and/or bottom of your box. Oil the foam lightly every now and then, and your stone will stay ready for use all the time.

I add one more thing to the boxes that I get with my stones: tiny hinges and a hasp to keep them closed. I know a big rubber band does the job just as well, but I'm never able to keep track of them in camp.

SHARPENING YOUR KNIFE

The hardest part of knife sharpening is keeping *exactly the same* angle of the blade to the stone throughout the entire sharpening process. Doing this is more important than the angle itself, although that's important, too.

The late John Jobson, that eminent outdoorsman whose opinions I value highly, maintained that the angle of inclination should be no more than about 10 degrees if you want a really keen edge. I won't disagree. I will say, though, that if you raise the spine of your knife no more than 8 or 10 degrees off the stone, you're going to be spending some time taking wire edges off your blade.

On the other hand should you increase the angle by upwards of 30 degrees, you'll have something more closely akin to a cleaver than a knife, and its slicing ability won't be anything you want to write home about.

Your own experimenting is the best guide to determining the sharpening angle that suits you best. My advice is to start at about 20 degrees, and go down from there if you want an edge that'll split a frog's hair. Much under 10 degrees, and you'll likely need a black surgical stone for finishing.

Before you begin your honing, oil your stone and let it soak for a couple of hours. (This is for

171

Correct honing stroke

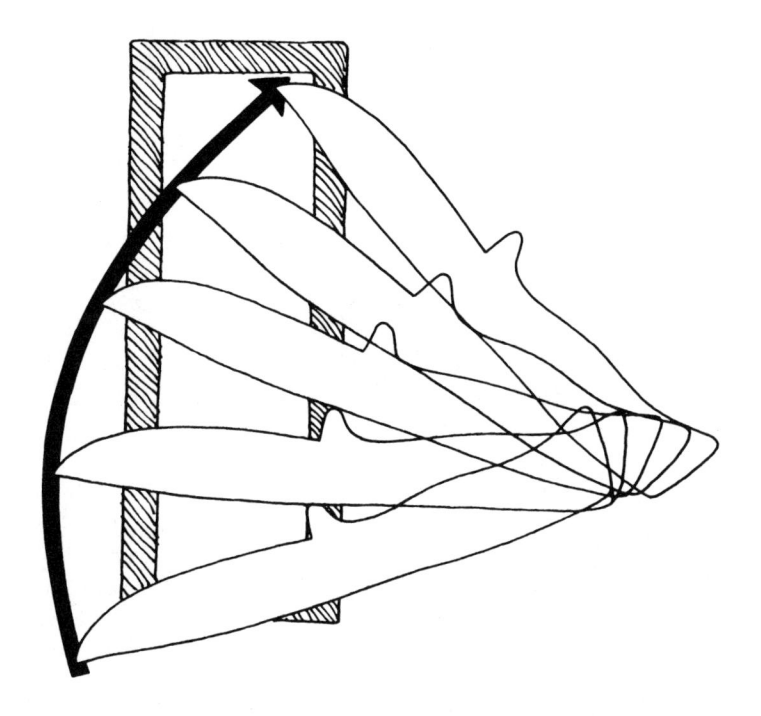

Correct blade-to-stone angle

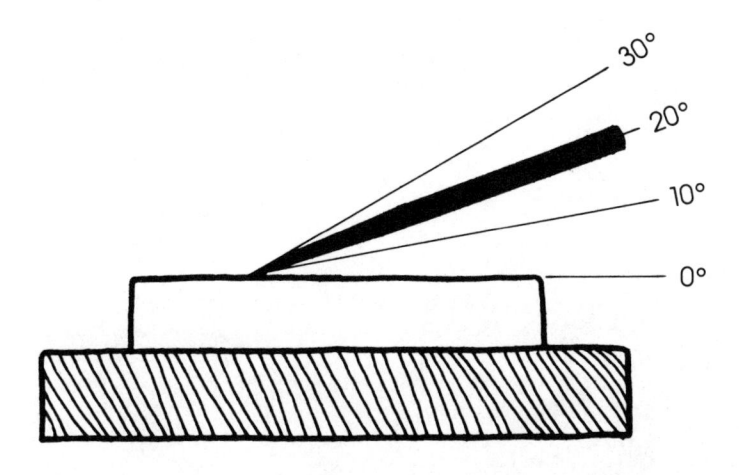

A. Honing stand, with oilstone in place, is clamped to the bench with "C" clamps.

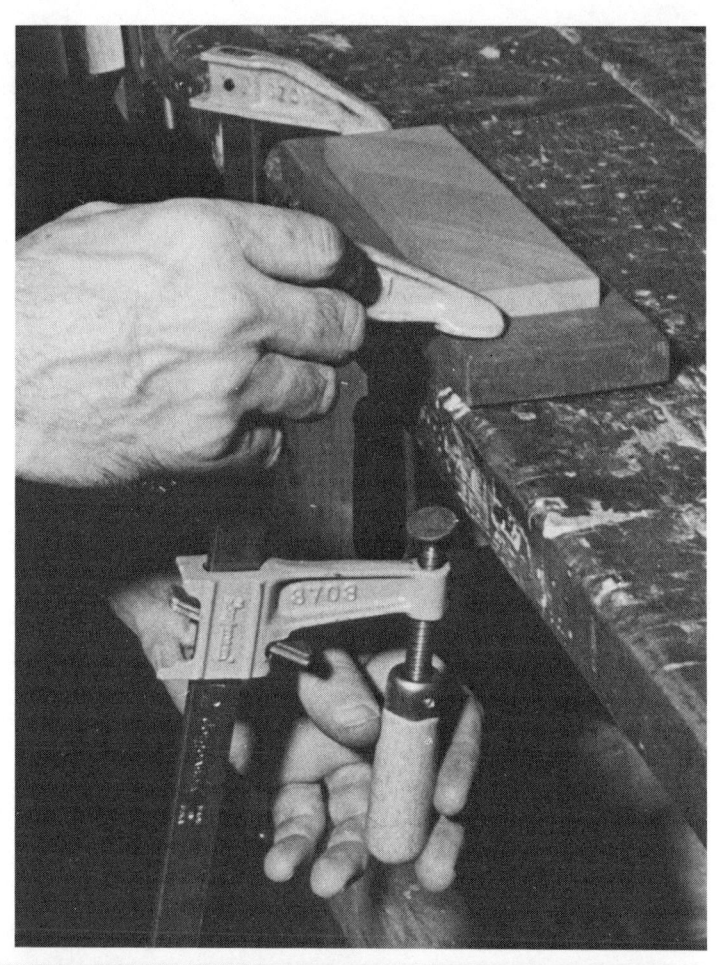

B. Light honing oil (author uses machine oil and kerosene mix) is squirted on the stone and spread evenly over it.

new stones, not those that have been used awhile.) Several good honing oils are on the market, but I find that a 50–50 mix of kerosene and light machine oil suits me fine and costs a lot less than the store-bought stuff. Never use your stone without plenty of oil, else you'll clog the pores and ruin its honing ability.

To begin sharpening, lay the flat of the blade on the stone, then raise the spine just enough so that a light placed overhead doesn't cast a shadow on the stone. (If you can see a shadow, your angle is too great; lower the spine.) This will approximate 18 to 20 degrees.

Beginning with the cutting edge toward you, and the heel (closest to the hilt) on the far end of the stone, draw the blade toward you in a slicing motion. Slice your knife the full length of the blade, ending with only the point on the stone. At the same time, traverse the full length of the stone. Not only does this make the job go faster, it also causes the stone to wear evenly.

As shown in the accompanying photographs, your master hand (the right unless you're left-handed) should hold the knife by its handle and guide it along its route. Your other hand should be placed just above the tip of the blade, with your

C. Correct blade angle (about 20 degrees) can be judged when shadow is no longer visible when viewed from above.

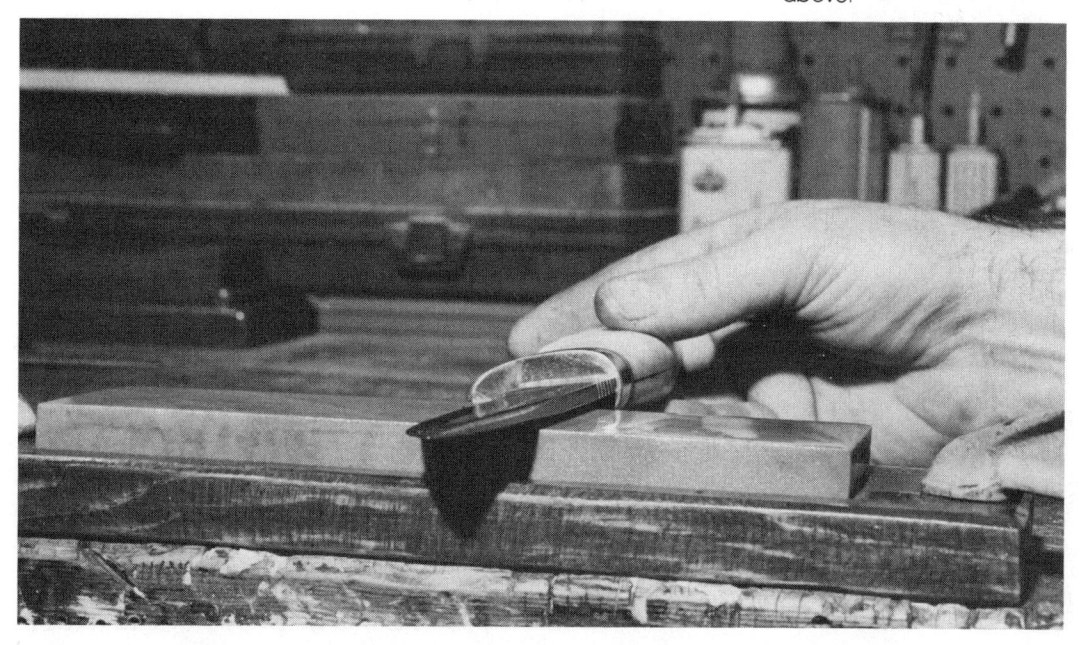

D. Begin honing with heel of knife on stone and slice knife away from you, as described in text.
E. Forward stroke is completed with just the point of the knife remaining on the stone.

fingertips overhanging just enough to feel the contact point between the blade and the stone. With a little practice this will enable you to judge almost instinctively the angle at which the blade is inclined.

The primary function served by the hand on the blade, however, is to enable you to maintain constant and equal pressure on the blade. Take care to retain the same amount of pressure as you come around the curve of the blade, by slightly raising the handle with your master hand. Keep fairly heavy pressure on the blade and take pains not to rock it. This, more than anything else, is the secret behind good knife sharpening. It takes a

F. Backstroke is begun with edge toward you and heel of knife on far end of stone.
G. Stroke is completed with just the point of the knife remaining on the stone.

little practice, but once you get the hang of it, you'll wonder how you ever did it wrong.

After you've made six or eight strokes across the stone with the cutting edge toward you, turn the blade over and use the same slicing motion an equal number of times on the other side. Again, you'll begin with the heel on the stone and complete your stroke at the tip. This time, of course, you'll be slicing the blade away from you, rather than toward you.

After alternately stroking each side a number of times, check the edge visually by sighting along it with the blade held toward the light. It's likely, at this point, that the curve and point will not be quite as sharp as the straight portion of the edge.

H. Razor edge is obtained by stropping on a strop dressed with oil and red rouge.

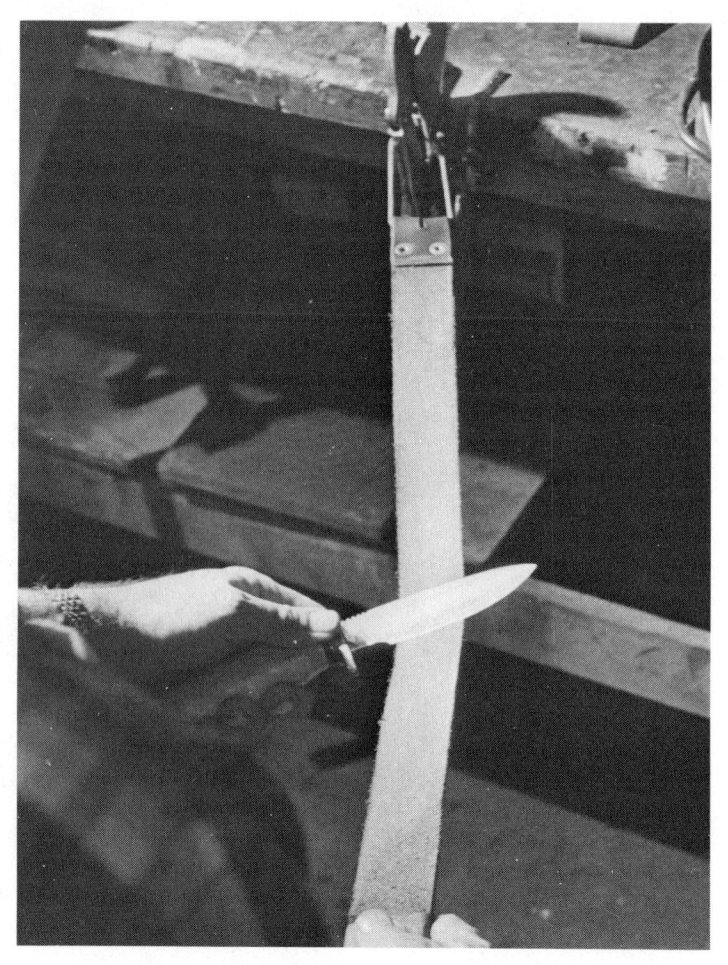

Repeat the operation, bearing down more on these areas, but completing your full stroke each time.

There are several methods of testing the final sharpness of your blade. The one I like best is to slice through a piece of typing paper held by one corner. Anywhere there's a rough or dull spot, the knife will stick or slide through without cutting. If the blade slices the paper cleanly, you've done your job well.

CARING FOR YOUR KNIFE

Most hunters and fishermen, being knowledgeable in the care of guns and tackle, know how to take good care of their fine knives. Leather attracts moisture, so it's best not to leave your blades sheathed over extended periods. I devote a shelf of my gun cabinet to knives, but still like to keep a few hanging on the walls of my basement office. I've found that a thin film of WD-40 is all that is required to keep them in good shape. Gun grease, which is what I used to use, has been outmoded.

Leather handles are a bit of a problem, because the same dryness that keeps your blades from rusting causes them to dry and shrink over a period of years. To prevent this, wipe the handles of your knives with neat's-foot oil or other leather preservative from time to time.

In addition to carrying your bench stone along on extended hunting and camping trips, it's good practice to carry a small pocket stone or sharpening steel to touch up your blade during a lengthy skinning job. Some sheaths are equipped with pockets for small stones. Such dual-purpose sheaths are a bit bulky for my tastes, and the pockets are generally too small to take a 4-inch stone. Instead, I like to make a small pouch-type case with flap for my stone, and carry it on my belt in back. I never know it's there until I need it.

There are several good sharpening steels on the market, the best of which I suppose are the ones coated with diamond dust. A friend gave me one, and I like the job it does. These things are fairly expensive, though, and as far as I can see, they don't do anything a good Arkansas pocket stone won't do for about half the price.

I can see they don't do anything a good Arkansas pocket stone won't do for about half the price.

I've taken so much kidding from my hunting buddies over my affinity for stropping blades that I'm a little reluctant to mention it. Still, if you don't mind a little good-natured ribbing, a strop is a sure-fire way to keep a really fine edge on a sheath knife. (Don't try it with a folding knife unless it's a lock-blade.)

Knives, like razors, are stropped spine first. I make my own strops from 2-inch strips of latigo or harness leather that I first oil with neat's-foot and then dress them with red rouge. This combination will remove a wire edge like nothing else I know.

When you get into knife-making, you tend to buy the equipment—like buffing wheels and polishers—that lets you care for your knives better than most outdoorsmen. There's no such thing as brass that won't tarnish or carbon steel that won't oxidize. A few turns on the buffing wheel will have 'em looking like new.

My non-knife-making friends have tumbled to this, and several of them are frequently asking me to polish their knives for them. I'm always glad to oblige; working with different knives and comparing their quality is part of the fun of knife-making.

APPENDIX

Glossary of Knife-Making Terms

A

AISI-SAE Classification System—An alphanumeric system developed by the Society of Automotive Engineers and the American Iron and Steel Institute for codifying the compositional limits of all steel.

Alloy steel—Steels to which alloying elements such as chromium, tungsten, molybdenum, etc. have been added to impart desired physical properties.

Anneal—A heat-treating process for softening and normalizing steel. It involves heating the metal to its approximate critical temperature point, then cooling slowly in a medium such as sand or lime.

Arkansas oilstone—A high-quality sharpening stone made from naturally occurring novaculite; especially that which comes from southwestern Arkansas.

Arkansas toothpick—A large dagger developed in the South and used by Confederate troops during the Civil War.

Austenite—A mode of steel that exists between the metal's upper and lower critical temperature points. Quenching takes place when steel reaches this mode during the hardening process.

B

Bench stone—A large (usually 2- by 8-inch) sharpening stone intended for use at the workbench. Such stones are clamped to the bench to permit two-handed sharpening.

Bolsters—Pieces of metal added to the handle immediately above the hilt to strengthen the knife and add to its attractiveness.

Bowie knife—A large clip-point fighting knife attributed to James Bowie (the designer) and James Black (the maker). Bowie knives influenced the design of straight knives used in America for almost a century.

Brass—A soft metal alloyed from copper and zinc. Frequently used for hilts and pommels, brass is available in cast or bar form.

Brittleness—A usually undesireable property of steel that permits no permanent distortion without breakage occurring. Some metals, such as cast iron, are extremely brittle.

Buffing compound—Any one of several formulations applied to buffing wheels, either in stick or liquid form, for finishing knife blades and other metals.

Buffing wheel—A disc-shaped wheel, usually of stitched muslin, used on rotary tools to finish metals and other hard materials. Buffing wheels come in various sizes from 4- to 10-inches.

Butt cap—A piece of soft metal affixed to the upper portion of the knife's tang; usually ¼-inch or more in thickness. (See *butt plate* and *pommel*.)

Butt plate—A thin piece of soft metal, usually ¼-inch or less in thickness, affixed to the upper portion of the tang.

C

"C" Scale—A measurement of hardness on the Rockwell tester which employs a diamond cone to indent the metal being tested, commonly used for showing knife-blade hardness.

Caping knife—A small, specialized skinning knife used for delicate work around an animal's head.

Carbon steel—A classification applied to all plain (non-alloy) steels in commercial use. Carbon steels are further classified according to the amount of carbon they contain, i.e. low-carbon, medium-carbon, or high-carbon.

Choil—A cutout for the index finger immediately below the hilt on some straight knives.

Clip-Point—A blade configuration characterized by a sharply inclined, almost straight drop from spine to point. In hunting knives, this design has lost some of its popularity in recent years.

Corrosion resistance—The ability of a steel to resist oxidation or rusting. "Stainless" is the term popularly applied to corrosion-resistant steels.

Cutler's rivet—A special-purpose two-piece rivet widely used for joining scale handles to the tang.

D

Dagger—A broad descriptive term applied to any of several double-edged, gradually tapered fighting knives. The dagger is among the oldest of knife designs.

Damascus steel—An ancient method of forging, developed by the Syrians for making knife and sword blades; it is characterized by numerous fine laminations which impart a wavy appearance to the blade.

Decalescence point—The temperature, in heat treating steel, at which pearlite transforms to austenite. Ordinary high-carbon steel reaches its decalescence point at 1,330 degrees F.

Dirk—Originally, a large dagger developed by the Scottish highlanders; today, a less precise term applied to several large, double-edged knives.

Double hilt—A hilt design characterized by two quillons. It is widely used on fighting knives.

Drawn—A synonymous term for tempered.

Drop-point—A blade configuration characterized by a gradually inclined, slightly curved drop from spine to point. Blades of this design, widely used in the 19th Century, have enjoyed a resurgence in recent years, largely at the expense of the clip-point design.

Ductility—The ability of a metal to be deformed without breaking. Soft metals are highly ductile as a rule; hard metals such as steel, less so.

Duraluminum—An alloy composed of 95 percent aluminum, 4 percent copper, and lesser amounts of manganese and magnesium. It is used by some knife manufacturers for hilts and pommels but is impractical for home hobbyists because of its age-hardening characteristics.

E

Edge—The cutting portion of the blade.

Elasticity—The ability of a metal to return to its original shape after being bent; it is a highly desirable property in knife blades.

Epoxy—A bonding agent composed of polymide or amine resin, to which is added a hardening agent which causes a chemical reaction to occur.

F

False edge—That portion of a clip-point blade that extends from the spine to the point; the term false edge is used only if the portion is unsharpened.

Finger clips—Indentations cut in the knife handle to accommodate the fingers. Clips cut in the upper portion of the blade are more correctly called choils.

Flux—A chemical agent used in connection with soldering and welding to remove oxide and help establish capillary action in the joint. Zinc chloride is a commonly used soldering flux.

Full annealing—An annealing process in which the steel is heated to just above its upper critical temperature point. (See *normalizing* and *process annealing*)

Full tang—A tang design characterized by metal which runs the full length and width of the handle; in this method of construction, scales or slabs are pinned or riveted to the tang.

G

Guard—In knife design, a synonymous term for hilt.

Green River blade—A descriptive term applied to knives designed and made by the John Russell Company beginning in the early 19th century; so named for the Green River of Massachusetts where the Russell factory (Green River Works) was located.

Grind—The method by which the edge is placed (ground) on a knife blade. About six different grinds are commonly recognized.

Grip—A synonymous term for handle.

H

Handle—That portion of the knife above the hilt and below the pommel, if present; otherwise (in full-tang construction) all of the knife above the blade.

Hardening—The process of heating steel above its lower critical temperature (decalescence) point, and then quenching in the proper medium such as brine, water, oil, or air.

Hardness—That physical property of metal which allows it to resist forcible penetration or plastic deformation. (See *Rockwell test.*)

Heat treatment—Any one of several processes applied to finished steel to impart desired physical properties. Primary heat-treating processes are annealing, hardening, and tempering.

High-alloy steel—A general classification for all steels in which the level of alloying elements exceeds 10 percent.

High-carbon steel—Carbon steel in which the level of carbon added exceeds .6 percent. Most of today's high-carbon steels contain at least .85 percent carbon.

Hilt—In knives, that portion which forms a platform for the user's hand between handle and blade; in swords, all of the weapon except the blade. The terms hilt and guard are synonymous in knives.

K

Kukri—The highly stylized fighting knife of the Nepalese Gurkha tribe; the blade is characterized by a sharp curve, with concave edge and convex spine.

Kris—The highly stylized fighting knife of the Malaysian tribes; the blade is characterized by a series of serpentine curves.

L

Laminated blade—A method of knife-blade construction characterized by a hard core and softer outer layers. Most laminated blades are imported from Norway. Such blades are distinctly different from Damascus blades, which contain multiple laminations of almost microscopic thickness.

Latigo—A type of vegetable-tanned, natural (undyed) cowhide that is particularly well suited to sheath making.

Lower critical temperature point—The lowest temperature at which a steel can be quenched to impart desired hardness.

M

Malleability—That property of metal which allows it to be hammered or rolled into other sizes or shapes. Heating increases the malleability of metal.

Martensite—A mode of steel that exists after it has been hardened and before it has been tempered; characterized by the needlelike pattern of its molecules.

Modified tang—A modification of the round-tang design, in which the upper portion of the tang is drilled rather than threaded.

N

Needle file—A general term used to describe any of several small files, the blades of which measure approximately 3 inches in length; used by knifemakers to slot hilts and other fine work.

Nickel silver—A white alloy composed of copper, zinc, and nickel. True nickel silver is harder and tougher than brass, but much of the nickel silver being sold today has a high percentage of zinc and relatively low percentage of nickel. The terms nickel silver and German silver are synonymous.

Novaculite—A metamorphic sandstone possessing, in its pure state, qualities which make it highly desirable as a sharpening stone. (See *Arkansas oilstone.*)

Normalizing—An annealing process for relieving internal stresses and strains caused by prior operations, such as forging.

P **Pearlite**—Steel that has not yet been subjected to the hardening process. It is characterized by a random molecular structure.

Pickling—A cleaning process in which untreated steel is dipped in acid to clean and protect it.

Pins—Short pieces of malleable metal (usually brass or copper) used to join knife parts, especially scales to tangs.

Point—The tip of the blade.

Polishing wheel—A disc-shaped wheel, usually of white felt, used on rotary tools to finish metals, particularly steel. Polishing wheels impart a higher, mirrorlike finish than do buffing wheels.

Pommel—A piece of soft metal, usually curved, affixed to the upper portion of the tang. Pommels are generally thought of as being larger and more prominent than butt plates or caps.

Process annealing—An annealing process in which the steel is heated to just below its lower critical temperature point.

Q **Quillon**—The crossbar on the hilt; depending on hilt design, either one or two quillon(s) may be present.

Quenching—The act of rapidly cooling steel during the hardening process to prevent it from passing through its recalescence point. Commonly used quenching media are air, water, oil, and brine.

R **Recalescence point**—That temperature at which steel, when being cooled, transforms its molecular structure to become softer and more ductile.

Ricasso—The unsharpened portion of the blade immediately below the hilt.

Rockwell test—A test applied to steel and other metals to measure their hardness. With steel, a diamond cone is used to gauge and record the metal's resistance to indentation under a load of 150 kg.

Rouge—A stick-type buffing and polishing compound applied to felt and muslin wheels to fine-finish steel and other hard materials. The most commonly used types of rouge are red, white, and brown.

Round tang—A tang design characterized by metal that is rectangular for most of its length, but rounded at the end. In most construction techniques using the round tang, the upper portion is threaded to receive a tapped pommel.

S

Sambar stag—Stag obtained from the large sambar deer of India and known variously as sambar, Indian, and imported stag. Nearly all commercial handle material available in the U.S. is from this deer.

Scale(s)—Known also as slabs, these relatively thin pieces of wood, stag, horn or synthetic are pinned or riveted to the tang in full-tang construction.

Short tang—A tang design characterized by metal that is approximately one-half to three-fourths the overall length of the handle. Short tangs, which can be adapted from any of the longer tangs, are used in blind-hole and inlet-scale construction.

Silver solder—A soldering alloy usually composed of 96 percent tin and 4 percent silver. It has a somewhat higher melting point than normal solder, and a significantly greater bonding strength.

Single hilt—A hilt characterized by a single quillon.

Sintered metal—An alloy, which may or may not contain steel, composed of powdered elements fused together under extreme pressure, but at temperatures below the melting point of most of its constituents. Stellite 6K is a sintered material that has been used to some extent for knife blades.

Slab—A synonymous term for scale.

Soft metal—A general description that includes all of the softer nonferrous metals. In knifemaking, the term usually refers to brass, aluminum, or nickel silver.

Spine—The thickest portion of the blade; in

single-edged knives, the back; in double-edged knives, the center portion or rib.

Stag—Antler material from any member of the deer family.

Stainless steel—A high-alloy steel that derives its ability to resist corrosion from relatively high concentrations of chromium, sometimes in combination with nickel.

Stick—A solid piece of handle material used in round-tang construction. The terms stick and block are synonymous in most usages.

Swedge—In clip-point blade design, the sharpened false edge. The Bowie knife popularized swedged blades for many years.

T

Tang—That portion of the knife that extends into or through the handle.

Tensile strength—A measurement of the maximum amount of pull that a material can withstand before breaking. Important in some metal applications, it is of little significance in knife construction.

Temper—The process of reheating hardened steel to a desired temperature below its lower critical temperature point, primarily to impart toughness.

Tool steel—A broad classification of steels used for tool-making that ranges from simple carbon compounds to compounds containing several different alloying elements. Although often used interchangeably, the terms *high-carbon* and *tool* are not precisely synonymous.

Toughness—The ability of metal to withstand shock or impact. Toughness is the opposite condition of brittleness and extremely important in knife blades.

U

Upper critical temperature point—The highest temperature at which a steel can be quenched to impart desired hardness.

W

Wall hanger—A semi-derisive term used to describe a knife that is too large, too expensive, or too fragile for any practical application. Many of today's collectors' knives are aptly so described.

Working knife—A knife designed and made to be used as a tool.

Where to Order What You Need

Here is a list of names and addresses of major suppliers. Their phone numbers are given where telephone orders are encouraged or accepted.

Atlanta Cutlery Corporation
911 Center Street
(PO Box 839)
Conyers GA 30207
Phone: (404) 922-3700
Send $1 for first catalog; thereafter, occasional orders keep you on their mailing list. Liberal discount policy for quantity orders.

Brookstone Company
125 Vose Farm Road
Peterborough NH 03458
Free catalog of workbench tools

Brownells Incorporated
Route 2, Box 1
Montezuma IA 50171
Phone: (515) 623-5401
Send $3 for catalog, refunded with order.

Craftsman Wood Service Company
2727 S. Mary Street
Chicago IL 60608
Send 50¢ for catalog of woods and woodworking tools.

Cherry Corners Mfg.
  Company
11136 Congress Road
Lodi OH 44254
Send self-addressed envelope for information.

E. Christopher Firearms
  Company
6818 State Road 128
  (PO Box 283)
Miamitown OH 45041
Phone: (513) 353-1321
Send $1 for specification sheets and knife-making booklet.

Custom Knifemaker's
  Supply
PO Box 308
Emory TX 75440
Phone: (214) 473-3330
Send $2 for catalog.

J. R. Fillinger
Route 1
Patriot OH 45658
Send 50¢ for catalog.

Indian Ridge Traders
306 S. Washington
  (PO Box 869)
Royal Oak MI 48068
Phone: (313) 547-6131
Free catalog and knife-making tips. Liberal discount policy for quantity orders.

Rigid Knives
9919 Prospect Ave.
  (PO Box 460)
Santee CA 92071
Write for free information and catalog.

A. G. Russell Company
1705 Highway 71 North
Springdale AR 72764
Phone: (501) 751-7341
Write for free catalog. Purchases may be placed on Master Charge or Visa.

N. Selvey
108 S. 11th Street
Blue Springs MO 64015
Write for prices and information.

Tandy Leather Company
PO Box 791
Fort Worth TX 76101
Write for free catalog.

Mike Wells
Sky Meadow
Spray OR 97874
Write for prices and information.

Knife-making Supplies and Services

Arkansas oilstones
  E. Christopher Firearms
  A. G. Russell

Aluminum bar stock
  J. R. Fillinger

Blades (factory and handground)
  Atlanta Cutlery
  Custom Knifemaker's Supply
  E. Christopher Firearms
  Indian Ridge Traders
  A. G. Russell

Brass bar stock
  Atlanta Cutlery
  Custom Knifemaker's Supply

Brass castings (hilts and pommels)
  Atlanta Cutlery
  E. Christopher Firearms
  Indian Ridge Traders

Buffing compound
  Brownells
  Cherry Corners Mfg. Co.

Buffing wheels (muslin)
  Brownells

Cutler's rivets
  Atlanta Cutlery
  E. Christopher Firearms
  Custom Knifemaker's Supply
  Indian Ridge Traders

Epoxy
  Custom Knifemaker's Supply

Heat-Treating Services
  J. R. Fillinger
  N. Selvey

Horn
  Custom Knifemaker's
    Supply
  E. Christopher
    Firearms

Imported stag
  E. Christopher
    Firearms
  Custom Knifemaker's
    Supply
  Atlanta Cutlery

Knife-making kits
  Atlanta Cutlery
  Indian Ridge Traders
  Rigid Knives
  A. G. Russell

Leather discs (pre-cut for handles)
  E. Christopher
    Firearms

Leather (for sheath-making)
  Tandy Leather

Leatherworking tools and supplies
  Tandy Leather

Micarta
  Atlanta Cutlery
  Custom Knifemaker's
    Supply
  E. Christopher
    Firearms

Native stag (deer and elk)
  Mike Wells

Nickel-silver bar stock
  Atlanta Cutlery
  Custom Knifemaker's
    Supply

Nickel-silver castings (hilts and pommels)
  Atlanta Cutlery
  Custom Knifemaker's
    Supply

Plexiglas (for spacers)
  Brownells

Polishing wheels (felt)
  Brownells

Screw-type rivets (for handles)
  E. Christopher
    Firearms
  Custom Knifemaker's
    Supply

Silver solder and flux
  Brownells
  Custom Knifemaker's
    Supply

Spacer stock
  Atlanta Cutlery
  Custom Knifemaker's
    Supply
  Indian Ridge Traders

Steel (for blade-making)
  Custom Knifemaker's
    Supply
  J. R. Fillinger

Tools and workbench items
  Brookstone Company
  Brownells

Wood (American and exotic)
  Atlanta Cutlery
  E. Christopher
    Firearms
  Craftsman Wood
    Service
  Custom Knifemaker's
    Supply
  Indian Ridge Traders

Woodworking tools
  Craftsman Wood
    Service